HEARTF...
LISTEN W...   ...T

"Offers those seeking love and abundance a place to start the process."
>—LINDA A. FIRESTONE, PH.D.
>author of *Awakening Minerva:*
>*The Power of Creativity in Women's Lives*

"Eileen Flanagan's book is a refreshing change. . . . It offers hope and a depth of guidance seldom seen. . . . I recommend her perspective and process to everyone in search of a mate."
>—HARVILLE HENDRIX, PH.D.
>bestselling author of *Getting the Love You*
>*Want and Keeping the Love You Find*

"Offers the reader a glimpse into the spiritual nature of relationships . . . a path toward wholeness. . . . A refreshing change from your typical 'how to find a mate' relationship book. Highly recommended."
>—JASON ELIAS
>coauthor of *Feminine Healing*

"A profoundly insightful book that challenges us all to examine ourselves and maybe even rethink what we mean when we say 'love.'"
>—RONN ELMORE, PSY.D.
>author of *How to Love a Black Woman*

LISTEN WITH YOUR HEART

SEEKING THE SACRED IN ROMANTIC LOVE

EILEEN FLANAGAN

WARNER BOOKS

A Time-Warner Company

Warner Books, Inc., 1271 Avenue of the Americas, New York, NY 10020
Visit our Web site at http://warnerbooks.com
Ⓦ A Time Warner Company

Printed in the United States of America
First Printing: January 1999
10 9 8 7 6 5 4 3 2 1

Library of Congress Cataloging-in-Publication Data

Flanagan, Eileen.
   Listen with your heart : seeking the sacred in romantic love / Eileen Flanagan.
      p.   cm.
   Portions of this work have previously appeared in several magazines from 1994–1997.
   ISBN 0-446-67448-6 (pbk.)
   1. Love.   2. Love—Religious aspects.   3. Man-woman relationships—Case studies.   4. Conduct of life.   I. Title.
BF575.L8F55   1999
306.7—dc21   98-14922
                                                                              CIP

Portions of this work have previously appeared in the following:

"God, Marriage and the Biological Clock," *Venture Inward* 10, no. 4 (July/August 1994): 23–25, 44.

"Wrestling with Love," *Venture Inward* 11, no. 4 (July/August 1995): 34–37.

"Is Love Scarce?" *Tikkun* 11, no. 6 (November/December 1996): 41–42, 53.

"Letting God Be the Matchmaker," *Gnosis*, no. 43 (spring 1997): 33–37.

"The Wisdom to Know the Difference," *Venture Inward* 13, no. 3 (May/June 1997): 20–22.

Book design by Giorgetta Bell McRee
Cover design & illustration by John Martinez

For my mother, Helen,
and my husband, Tom

Acknowledgments

$\mathcal{W}$riting this book has been an experience of trusting the guidance of the Spirit. I have been blessed along the way by the help of many people. First, I owe a huge debt to all of the women and men whom I interviewed. I was touched by their openness and generosity in telling me their stories. Many things people said during interviews have remained with me, enriching my life as much as they have enriched the book. Because some asked to remain anonymous and others asked only that their first names be used, I will not name those interviewed here. I simply offer them my thanks.

I owe a general thanks to friends from Pendle Hill, particularly the many people who encouraged me to keep writing after I presented an initial essay on this topic. Many read early drafts of the manuscript and offered helpful feedback and encouragement. I am especially grateful to Mary Gabel, Marcelle Martin, Rebecca Mays, and Lucy Sherman for their detailed editorial suggestions. A. Robert Smith, the editor of *Venture Inward* magazine, and Jane Dreifus-Smith have been continually supportive. I thank my mother, Helen Flanagan, who helped me pay the rent when I decided to quit my job to write full time, as well as Sue Burrus and Patty Nesbitt, who also offered material support when it was needed.

Thanks to my agent, Sheree Bykofsky, who did a great job finding a home for this book, and her assistant, Janet Rosen, who gave helpful suggestions for improving the manuscript. My editors at Warner Books were a delight to work with, offering constructive guidance and enthusiastic support; I am particularly grateful to Diane Stockwell, Jessica Papin, and Amy Einhorn.

Of course a very special thanks goes to my husband, Tom Volkert. His presence in my life provided much of the experience on which this book is based. Not only did he agree to have parts of his own story put into print, but he was also gracious enough to read draft after draft of the whole manuscript. In addition to all the ways he supported this project, I thank him most of all for our lives together.

Contents

LISTEN WITH YOUR HEART

Introduction: Searching for Courtship

$\mathcal{W}$e were browsing through Borders bookstore on a Saturday night as Jayne updated Nancy on the status of her new relationship. Wandering past the self-help section, a title caught my eye that I just couldn't resist: *Searching for Courtship: The Smart Woman's Guide to Finding a Good Husband.* The three of us, all heterosexual women in our early thirties, formed a giddy huddle in the aisle and began thumbing through the pages.

Friendships with men "divert you from your higher goal," says Winnifred B. Cutler, Ph.D. "If you have time to spare after scheduling your three search events per week, you would probably do better to build friendships with other women—unless your male friend fixes you up with courtship candidates." Cutler advocates a systematic program for finding a husband, using a loose-leaf binder, two inches thick, and a set of twelve dividers to track different sources of male suitors. Nancy was particularly amused by the binder and began speculating on how one might have

1

helped her track down her new husband, Rick, who was a few aisles away thumbing through baseball books.

We began to giggle uncontrollably, like fourth graders looking at nude pictures in the locker room. Jayne's boyfriend, Matt, wandered over but quickly disappeared, perplexed by our hysterical laughter. The longer we stood mocking the book, however, the more I got the sinking feeling its message was not so funny, or distant. I grew quiet as we headed out of the store—Nancy and Rick, Jayne and Matt, and I, the odd number, as usual. The warning rang out loud and clear. Better hurry up; all the good ones are almost gone!

At the time I was thirty-one, never married, and well aware of the pressure single women face. My mother hinted that she hoped she'd live to see her grandchildren. An old friend said she was sad I didn't have "someone special." Although I had enjoyed my single twenties, *Searching for Courtship* hit a nerve. I bristled at the sexist assumptions and the clinical approach to dating, but I laughed in nervous recognition. The book compelled me to examine the ways I was searching for courtship and the assumptions I held about love.

I returned to the bookstore alone and found numerous guides on how to find a lover or mate: *How to Start a Romantic Encounter, 50 Ways to Find a Lover,* and *Guerrilla Dating Tactics.* Exploring other stories, I realized how many books on the market explicitly promise marriage: *How to Get Married in a Year or Less, How to Marry the Man of Your Choice,* and *How to Marry the Rich,* to name just a few. I began noticing courtship advice throughout the media: television talk shows on "How to Meet that Future Spouse" and magazine articles on "Shopping for a Man." The shopping approach showed up again and again, from newspaper classifieds where people advertise their height, weight, and hobbies to dating services where people pay exorbitant fees, hoping to buy "love."

Most popular dating advice reflects a consumer approach to love. We are told that finding a mate is like "shopping for a car or an apartment," and we should begin by writing a checklist of what we want. Dating guides tell us to advertise our assets by wearing sheer black pantyhose and short skirts. In the marriage market, we are merchandise as well as consumers, selling ourselves in exchange for what we want. As one book puts it, "The trick is to have such a clear assessment of the package you are buying that you can feel confident you got the better deal on balance."

Describing marriage as a business deal reveals the basic selfishness of the consumer approach to love. The whole point of the shopping list is to determine "What do I want?" The question "What can I give?" is only asked to evaluate my bargaining position, to list the assets I can use as bait to attract a lover. This approach misses the essence of real love: the joy of caring about another's well-being and happiness. It is the unselfishness of love that expands and fulfills us, that challenges us to grow and become more. It is a sad irony that so many books promote narcissism in the name of love, steering their readers away from the real wonder of loving.

The hope for love is human and good. There is nothing wrong with wanting to find a life partner, and by criticizing the courtship manuals, I am not criticizing the millions of women who have read them. I cannot mock a longing that I myself have known. The problem is that most courtship manuals speak to our fears rather than our hopes. They teach us to sell ourselves rather than be true to ourselves. They promote manipulation rather than real loving.

These books are not anomalies we can dismiss by saying, "Well, *I* don't read that sort of thing." Their assumptions permeate our culture, affecting how we approach intimate relationships even when we think we are working out of a different value system. That is why I take the courtship manuals seriously, even while I laugh at their more ludicrous suggestions. Studying these books forced me to realize how often I have advertised my eyes and legs and calculated the timing of my sales pitch. I have browsed parties like a shopper cruising the mall, treating men like merchandise. I have written a shopping list. Recognizing these attitudes within myself and our culture challenged me to articulate a different vision.

At the time I began writing about these issues, I was living and working at a contemplative center founded by Quakers, and the spiritual values of this community provided a striking contrast to the consumer approach to love. As I struggled to accept the end of an important romance, I wondered how I could apply spiritual principles to my own romantic dilemmas. I was not seeking a profitable deal, but a partnership grown organically out of love, where the priority was to support and challenge each other to grow to our fullest potential. I knew this image was not a thing, to be achieved or purchased, but a way of living. How does one grow toward this way of living? I wondered. How can I admit I would like to share my life with someone without becoming a husband hunter? I began writing about these questions during Advent, the Christian season of waiting, and the theme of expectant waiting seemed to capture what I felt was the alternative to frantic man-hunting. Not passively sitting home feeling sorry for myself waiting, but instead actively waiting—living fully in the present, trusting that if I was meant to be married then it would happen without my forcing it.

I spent the next few years exploring ideas about love, reading widely in religion, psychology, and popular culture. Since women are the major audience for most how-to-catch-a-mate strategies, I focused on women's experience, although I hope the ideas in this book will resonate with men as well. I interviewed people I thought had something wise to say on the subject, thirty-nine women and men who shared their stories with extraordinary depth and candor. Often there was remarkable serendipity in the timing of the interviews, raising issues just when a person needed to talk about them or just when I needed to hear what they had to say.

My method of finding people to interview was very intuitive. Names were suggested to me. People appeared. The result was an interview sample that is disproportionately white, female, educated, and middle class. Most are from a Judeo-Christian background, though not all would consider themselves religious. I do not claim they are representative of our society as a whole. They do, however, represent a broad range of relationship experience. Some are married, several for the second time. Among the unmarried, some plan to remain single, while others hope to find a spouse someday. Some are sexually active. Some are celibate. Some are heterosexual. Some are lesbians. What all the people interviewed have in common is the desire to make decisions about their lives consciously and with integrity.

The most important research for this book was very personal, as I sought to live the questions I was asking. During the writing of this book, a friendship that began platonically developed into an intimate partnership, and chapter topics presented themselves through real-life dilemmas. As this relationship grew toward marriage, I became even more convinced that the way we approach courtship determines the quality of partnership we develop. A twelve-section binder could not have helped me find Tom. "Guerrilla dating tactics" could not have led to the mutually supportive partnership we share today. Rather than an achievement or a reward, our marriage is a gift, a grace, and a cause for gratitude.

What follows includes my story, as well as the stories of people I interviewed, contrasted with the consumer approach to love. In chapter 1, I present loving as a spiritual practice that enables us to grow closer to the Divine. In chapter 2, I show how the practice of spiritual discernment can guide us in this process, helping us find the form of loving that reflects our true selves. Chapter 3 explores the pressures that may muddy our discernment, such as fear, loneliness, and the biological clock. Chapter 4 examines the challenge of letting go and trusting in the search for love. Chapters 5 and 6 look at the development of romantic relationships and the issues that arise when two people attempt to discern if they are meant to marry. The conclusion points toward the future, reminding us that marriage is a continuing journey, not a final destination.

Unlike some authors, I do not promise a "marriage made in heaven" for those who follow my advice. There is no simple formula that will *make* someone fall in love with us, much as we may wish for one. There is no quick fix to loneliness, no foolproof plan to find our soul mate, and books that promise such easy answers merely distract us from the difficult but more gratifying work of searching our own souls. Ironically, inward searching may actually lead to more fulfilling relationships than searching for a mate. Several women I interviewed noted that it was only when they stopped looking for Mr. Right and focused on their own inner growth that meaningful relationships developed in their lives. This makes sense since a woman at peace with herself is more attractive than one who is desperate for affection. More important, a woman who knows who she is has more to offer than one who is looking for a partner to define and fulfill her. Any partnership she develops will be more loving than a marriage built on desperation and deception.

If we want a partnership with spiritual depth, we must begin by realizing that "shopping for a man" will not get us there. A dating strategy that is selfish and manipulative will attract selfish, manipulative people and lead to an unloving relationship. The means determine the ends. A thistle seed will not produce roses. Product and process are inseparable.

We can plant the seeds of anxiety and manipulation or the seeds of love and trust. This book is about learning to love and trust.

CHAPTER ONE

Abundant Love

I view my marriage as a spiritual path, a way of life that expands and fulfills me, that teaches me about myself and others, that brings me closer to God. This growth is usually not glamorous. It is the ordinary things that teach the most: deciding who changes the next diaper or who gets the last bagel, knowing when to speak and when to listen, learning to give of myself without giving up my self. Although I am still a beginner on this path, I know that my marriage is teaching me to be more generous and patient, in short, to be more loving.

For me, the process of waiting for the right partner and discerning whether or not we were meant to marry was itself full of growth. It involved letting go of some of my old ideas about relationships. It involved learning to listen more consciously to my inner voice for guidance. It involved admitting my own longing and learning to trust that my real needs would be met, though maybe not in the way I expected. A crucial step in this process was rejecting the consumer view of love. As long as I thought of love as a thing I had to find, I feared I would be love-poor. But when I shifted my focus to real loving—the process of creating love—I began to trust that the love in my life would always be plentiful, whether or not I ultimately married.

LOVE IS A VERB

"You will always have plenty of love," says Sharon, an energetic, joyful woman in her mid-forties. "That was the message most people needed to hear." Sharon had led a weeklong workshop on women's spirituality, and during the closing ritual participants had been invited to give each other the message they wished they had received as children. Without planning, most participants shared a similar message, the promise that love would be plentiful rather than scarce. For Sharon, whose mentally ill mother was physically and emotionally absent for much of her childhood, it had taken many years to learn to trust in love's abundance, and she was struck that so many workshop participants from different backgrounds needed the same assurance. Sharon recalls, "Hearing that message, 'You will always have plenty of love,' whispered in your ear repeatedly was an incredible gift!"

Most of us do not grow up assured of love's abundance. We believe we have to do something to deserve love, like an allowance we receive only after we've done our chores. Particularly in romantic love, we fear we have to dress a certain way, maintain a certain weight, or play a certain game in order to win another's heart. This message is reinforced by many of the self-proclaimed relationship experts who tell us we must follow a "love plan" or a set of rules if we have any chance of competing in the love market.

Magazines and dating manuals frequently use market language, telling us how to "advertise" our assets and "make the right sales pitch at the right time." *Haven't You Been Single Long Enough?* asks, "What is an advertiser's objective? To persuade and motivate someone to choose his product or service." "It's nothing more than supply and demand," states *The Great American Man Shortage and Other Roadblocks to Romance*. Many authors hook their largely female audience with questionable statistics about the scarcity of marriageable men. Highly successful women, we are told, have a disadvantage because men prefer to "marry down" the economic ladder; black women have it harder than white women partly because black men marry interracially at four times the rate of black women; and all women face diminishing odds as they get older and have to compete with younger women and widows. "Wake up!" warns *How to Marry the Man of Your Choice*. Unless you act now, "all you can look forward to is menopause, and a pet cat for companionship."

The belief that love is a commodity, like rubies or radium, with a limited supply, is one of the most toxic ideas in our culture. As long as we think of love as a noun—something that can be found, possessed, or lost—people will have to compete for it. There will be rich and poor. But when we think of love as a verb, an activity rather than a thing, love is as plentiful as we make it. This subtle shift in perception allows us to see the abundant potential for loving in our lives.

The author who clarified this distinction for me was Erich Fromm, a psychoanalyst and profound social thinker. In *To Have or to Be*, Fromm described *having* and *being* as

HAVING mode — seek security through possess
Being mode — Focus on what we are rather
the what have

12 *Eileen Flanagan*

two alternative ways of living. In the having mode, we try to make ourselves feel secure through possession. We are worth what we have: manicured lawn, beautiful children, advanced degree, executive office. In the being mode, what we have is unimportant. What we *are* is all that counts.

If we live in the having mode, as much of our culture does, we will try to grab love, to make it ours. We will think of it as something we must pursue when we don't have it and hold on to when we do. But Fromm asserted that love is not a thing that can be possessed: "In reality, there exists only the *act of loving*. To love is a productive activity. It implies caring for, knowing, responding, affirming, enjoying." True love does not mean possessing another's affections, and it cannot exist when our primary concern is receiving love. Rather, as Fromm defined it, "*Love is the active concern for the life and the growth of that which we love.*"

Love
is
Active
concern
for the
other,

This definition clarifies the difference between loving and trying to acquire love. Wearing a short skirt won't make us loving. Neither will cosmetic surgery. Such tactics are aimed at making someone love or desire us. They do not show an active concern for the life and growth of the other. Loving another means giving, not as a means to receiving, but for the other's sake. It may mean encouraging his decision to quit work and go back to school even though it will strain our finances. It may mean supporting her hunger for more solitude rather than forcing the closeness we desire. It may even mean letting our beloved say good-bye if that is what will foster her life and growth. Loving means giving when it is hard to give, not just when it is easy or convenient.

Loving does not require saying yes to everything our beloved asks. As the slogan "Friends don't let friends drive drunk" suggests, sometimes the most loving action is saying no even though it risks another's anger. Setting limits is more loving than lazy indulgence. Likewise, acknowledging discord is more loving than false sameness. Loving doesn't mean always agreeing; it means being honest and respectful about disagreements. Becoming a doormat for another person does not foster his or her growth, and it does little to foster our own. Loving ourselves, nurturing our own development, is part of being a loving person.

For example, learning to say "My feelings are hurt" was a huge step for me in relationships. I used to hide my tears, believing a fake smile was kinder than honesty. I was actually protecting myself, denying men the opportunity to know the real me. By holding back the vulnerabilities I feared were unattractive, I avoided the growth that can come through conflict. Gradually, I am learning to change this pattern. When I shared an early draft of this chapter with my partner, Tom, he gave me feedback I found discouraging. Rather than hiding my hurt, I let out all the tears, fears, and impatience of a frustrated writer. Tom listened. My outburst enabled him to appreciate my writing process and learn how to be more supportive; it helped me understand my own needs. By the end of the conversation, we both felt much closer. Feeling loved and appreciated, I was then able to hear the substance of his criticisms, which were very helpful in writing the second draft. In this situation, we were both loving. If Tom had merely said, "The chapter is great, honey," he would not have helped me grow as a writer. Likewise, if I had not shared my vulnerabilities, I would not have helped him grow as a lover. By sharing our true thoughts and feelings without blaming each other, we fostered growth in our relationship as well.

Sometimes we deny our painful emotions, believing this to be loving. We pretend not to mind when he spends every

Behaviors, on the surface, can seem loving but actually manipulative — wry to get approval

date describing the villainy of his ex-wife. We smile as we suffer through her son's first violin recital. We act cheerful as we clean up after a party for his friends. The ideal of cheerful servitude is another false image of love, one particularly ingrained in women. This behavior is often just another manipulation strategy, however. If we clean up the beer bottles in order to win his approval and affection, we are not being truly loving. We are merely trying to get him to love us—advertising generosity as we attempt to make a deal. This is very different from cleaning the party mess out of a simple desire to give, without any sense of martyrdom or proving our worth. The same action can be manipulative or loving depending on our inner motivation.

Sex, for example, can have very different meanings depending on our motivations. We may feel giving a partner pleasure gives us a certain power over him, enabling us to secure other things we want, such as affection, commitment, or fidelity. We may pursue a sexual relationship purely for our own pleasure, where sexual favors are simply assets to be traded on the love market. Or we may wish to give our partner physical pleasure, not for what we'll get in return, but for our beloved's sake. The exchange of lovemaking may be a wonderful expression of mutuality, helping lovers see beyond their own individual needs and desires and expanding their capacity to love.

Learning to recognize our real and often mixed motivations is an important part of learning to love. Our behavior may be influenced by unconscious fears and desires, and the difficult process of drawing these to the surface can help us see when we are being loving and when we are being manipulative. However, we should not postpone loving others until we are fully conscious and perfectly self-actualized. We never will be. Self-awareness, like loving, is a lifelong process. Indeed loving others is a powerful way to discover our own depth. Even our failed attempts to love can help us become more aware of our shadow side. In turn, the more honestly we know ourselves, including our own weaknesses, the more honestly we will be able to love ourselves and others. Learning to love and learning to know ourselves are ongoing processes that enhance each other, bringing us more in touch with our divine core.

TRANSCENDENCE

I recall times in my twenties when I showered men with affection and kindness, believing myself to be loving. I listened to their problems and pretended to understand. I did little errands for them. I sent sentimental notes. I was not desperate to get married. I just wanted adoration, and I hoped they would give it to me if I was sweet, generous, and entertaining enough. Of course, I tried to hide my need. I once drove around a city block three times in rush-hour traffic to avoid arriving early for a date, not wanting to appear too eager. The next week, I spent hours wondering whether to call the guy to say I had a good time or wait to see if he called me. He never called.

Looking back, I realize I wanted a boyfriend to fill the hole at the center of my life. I was growing disillusioned with the debt-ridden nonprofit where I worked. Unable to share these feelings with my coworkers, I felt increasingly isolated. I dreamed romance would refocus my energies and give my life new meaning. I thought a man would end my loneliness. I became intently aware of the men I passed in the supermarket, the bookstore, the gym. I scanned them like dresses in a department store display, trying them on in my imagination. The most stressful part was trying to sell myself. The few dates I had during this time felt like job interviews. I tried to impress them with my superior girlfriend qualifications and went home lonelier than before.

After one such disappointing experience, I took my dog and headed to the mountains for a week of solitude. This began a process of turning within for solace, refocusing my life from the inside out. I realized I had lost touch with my inner core, that quiet center that bonds me to the rest of creation. That was why I felt so alienated. I struggled to put words to this experience and gradually realized that rather than my job or my dating strategy, it was my relationship with God that was lacking. At first, I resisted using the word *God* because it conjured up an image of the Lincoln Memorial (an old white man looking down from a throne), an image I long ago rejected. I tried other words—Higher Power, Universe, Great Spirit, Goddess. For a while I wrote in my journal about the "Great Something," but that was too clumsy for the poet in me. Tentatively I began using the word *God*, careful not to ascribe it the pronoun *He.*

I now envision God as the unseen source that connects all beings, as groundwater links forest and field. When we love, we affirm our deep connectedness. We open a channel to the source and are refilled like a fresh spring well. In contrast, when we act out of fear and selfishness—operating from the having mode—we reinforce our illusion of separateness. We cut off the source, alienating ourselves from God and others.

Sometimes we try to manipulate God with the same market strategies we use on people. We suggest a deal—"I'll never skip services again if you send me a husband"—and confuse this with devotion. But God can't be manipulated. Opening to the sacred source means letting go of our wish lists and trusting we will be given all we need. It means for-saking the having mode and adopting the being mode. It means trusting in life's abundance. This message can be found in many spiritual traditions, as in the Gospel passage where Jesus tells his disciples not to be anxious about their lives, pointing to the birds of the air which are fed and the lilies of the field which are beautifully clothed. Zen Bud-dhism offers a similar message: live in the moment; stop sweating the small stuff.

This type of radical trust is difficult to practice. Our cap-italist culture teaches scarcity, competition, and faith in hard work. We grow up believing everything we receive is the result of our own earnest efforts, including love. Al-though I've adopted a lilies-of-the-field approach to mate-rial concerns—choosing meaningful jobs over profitable ones—I've been less trusting of love, particularly romantic love. That's been the one area of my life where I always felt anxious, believing that if I didn't run after love, it would never find me. On a deep level, I feared I would always be love-poor.

Reading the courtship manuals, I realized how they play on such fears—fear of loneliness, fear of being an old maid, fear of never having children. Relying on fate is described as "haphazard, inefficient, and unnecessary," and we are cau-tioned not to believe in magic or (it is implied) God. In-stead, we must have faith in the author's advice. *The Rules: Time-Tested Secrets for Capturing the Heart of Mr. Right* promises "a marriage truly made in heaven" for the faithful. The authors proclaim, "*The Rules* way is not a hobby, but a religion. We keep doing *The Rules* until the ring is on our finger!"

The claim that *The Rules* way is "a religion" is revealing. This religion is merely a list of rules followed in order to receive a reward—instead of heaven itself, a marriage "made in heaven." For me, religion is not a way to make deals with God; it is a way to let ourselves be guided and shaped by the source of all love. Religion is like the well that helps us reach the groundwater. It is not the source itself; it is a path to the source. Comparing *The Rules* to religion reveals another truth about today's secular culture: we worship romantic love in place of God. The wedding ring is a modern golden calf, an idol we dance around, hoping it will save us.

In *We: Understanding the Psychology of Romantic Love*, Jungian psychologist Robert A. Johnson argues that in Western culture romantic love has "supplanted religion as the arena in which men and women seek meaning, transcendence, wholeness, and ecstasy." This explains why we pursue romance so fervently, cling to it so tightly, and feel so disappointed when it fails to save us. If having a lover or spouse is perceived to be the only way we can experience union, it's no wonder we are so desperate. We long to feel connected to something greater than ourselves. When we seek a partner merely to fill our own emptiness, however, we are not really loving, not really reaching beyond ourselves. A relationship in which two people use each other to mask their loneliness will not ultimately provide the transcendence they seek.

A romantic relationship can help us experience transcendence, as long as we don't make the relationship itself the object of our worship. A deep connection to another person can help us feel connected to all of creation. We see the Divine reflected in our beloved and feel our own divine core uplifted by our partner's love for us. When we think of love as a commodity, there is always a price to be paid. The more I give my partner, the less I have for myself or others. But when love flows through us from the sacred source, then new possibilities become imaginable. Because there is enough love to go around, we never need to ration it. Romantic love becomes an expression of the sacred rather than a substitute for it.

For Sharon, learning to trust that she will always have plenty of love profoundly changed her approach to relationships. Having grown up in an affectionless family, Sharon says that for the first half of her life she lived with a feeling of scarcity, but a powerful experience in nature helped to recircuit her thinking. One day, she stood just below the edge of a lake with water spilling over the top. "I caught water in my hands, and I didn't need to cup it and hold it all. I could see all the water in the world in that lake. I could see the whole system coming, and I *knew* what abundance was like. Once my body got the message of abundance—and it came from the water spilling through my open hands—I felt that I would never clutch again. I would never have to live in a scarcity model." Sharon states, "I now trust in the abundance of the universe."

Sharon relates this trust to romantic love. "Now, choosing to be in a relationship, I'm more able to keep my focus on the All-of-it, which is the sacred for me. I'm not coming from a place of deficit. I'm coming from a place of abundance. Having a primary partner the way my life is structured now is just a complete gift." She looks upward and says, "I wasn't looking for this. And thank you!" Sharon says her romantic relationship with Mary Amanda feeds her work promoting women's art and culture. "I have more to give my work, more to give my community, more to give wherever I am." Sharon explains that intimacy fosters a powerful energy between partners that can get locked inside a relationship. "Whenever that flow is happening with us, our first response is to start to share it with other people. It's a different way of relating than I've had in the past. We're not looking into each other's eyes, saying, 'Aren't we having a good time here?' We're saying, 'What can we do now to share this?' "

MARRIAGE AS A SPIRITUAL PATH

When marriage is seen as a spiritual path, it expands our ability to love, benefiting more than just two partners. It may serve as a nurturing environment for children. Or it may offer one or both partners the support needed to perform socially beneficial work. Marriage may enable two people to consciously nurture each other's life and growth, so all they do is enhanced by their relationship. In this way, marriage enables them individually and as a couple to give more to the world around them.

While in her twenties, quiet and down-to-earth Judy considered living a single life of service to God, feeling that family life and a life of service were incompatible. Now married four years, she sees how her marriage to Michael enables her to serve God in ways she might not have attempted if she were single, such as becoming a long-term foster parent. Referring to their seven-year-old foster son, Judy reflects, "Taking Romanze down to the park to play, or up and down the street roller-skating, having fun with him, is helping the world, but it doesn't look that way. It's not what I had pictured before as helping the world. But if you're really going to be a parent and really be serious about it, that's what you're doing."

Patricia, who leads couples enrichment workshops with her husband, Brad, is enthusiastic about the ways her own marriage has helped her flourish. Now in her mid-forties,

Patricia's dark eyes sparkle as she states: "At every turn I can think of when there was something I wanted to do or try or work through, Brad's position was, 'Go for it! You can do it.' So I have felt throughout my marriage, which is now almost twenty-three years, that I've been empowered by it." Patricia notes that she and Brad have not confined themselves to rigid gender roles. "We've easily passed back and forth who's the primary breadwinner," she explains. "In 1978, for him to stay home and take care of our infant daughter while I went back to work was something we had to continually give one another permission for because the permission wasn't there in the culture."

Their marriage also includes the freedom to follow their individual spiritual journeys at separate paces. Although spirituality was important to Patricia from the beginning of their marriage, it was not central to Brad. Patricia states, "We were married thirteen or fourteen years when some things happened for him that fostered his spiritual development, and now that's something that is much more shared by the two of us." She is delighted by this change in him but recognizes that he had to make this journey at his own pace.

Patricia and Brad do not seek "meaning, transcendence, wholeness, and ecstasy" in each other. Instead they seek support for a lifetime of searching. This distinction allows a healthy space in their marriage, enabling each of them to deepen the individual process of self-discovery which in turn nurtures their togetherness. Space allows partners to see themselves and each other more clearly. Space enables them to confront their own incompleteness. Space leaves room for each one's individual connection to God. Ironically, it is only in our individuality that we can really experience union with others or the Divine. If we attempt to suppress our uniqueness in the name of partnership, we will stunt the relationship as well as ourselves.

When we see marriage as a spiritual path, our partner's uniqueness can teach us important life lessons. Accepting our lover's vulnerabilities can teach us compassion. Respecting another's rhythms can teach us patience. Understanding another way of thinking can broaden our perspective. The inevitable differences between two people will cause friction, but if we are open, honest, and committed to the struggle, the friction can polish us, as two gems in a tumbler polish each other.

Marcia, a Reconstructionist rabbi in her mid-forties, has studied both scripture and psychology. Speaking in the measured tone of a teacher, she offers a description of marriage that integrates the ancient understanding of her tradition with the insights of modern psychology. "For me, being partnered is a context for the evolution of my own spiritual growth," she states. "But even more than that, it is itself a spiritual practice." She explains that in Judaism, marriage is considered an important *mitzvah*, a spiritual imperative that brings people closer to God, like keeping the Sabbath and learning Torah.

Rabbi Marcia explains that marriage is one of the metaphors through which the Jewish people conceptualize their relationship with God: "We bind ourselves to a certain caliber of dynamic and intimate relationship with God that is one of love, and, as in a marriage, also sometimes one of wrestling. Like in a marriage, there is give and take and even sometimes struggle." Rabbi Marcia relates this to the name *Israel*, pronounced *Yisra'el* in Hebrew, which means "God-wrestler." This was the name earned by the patriarch Jacob, who wrestled with an angel of God and prevailed. "When we called our people *Yisra'el*, the "God-wrestlers," we recognized the implications. We wrestle with God with the intimacy of lovers. So too, we observe that in our most personal loving relationships we can experience a most profound God-wrestling. In the intimacy of partnered life, we experience a reflection of our relationship with God."

Marcia says of her own marriage, "I'm thrilled to be in a partnership, and I am thrilled with my partner. We love and wrestle a lot. We complement each other. We support each other. We challenge each other's edges, even in the times of friction. We are each stretched in our encounter with each other's unique perspective. In that encounter, which is framed by love and commitment, there is safety and risk in a tango. For myself, my marriage is an opportunity to grow spiritually and emotionally. I become more."

Being in a heterosexual relationship, Marcia explains, offers the particular opportunity to experience life from a different gender vantage point. She says, "For me as a woman, there is something about maleness that is radically 'other.' I find myself continually challenged to expand my awareness, to embrace the other. This can be at once completing, fulfilling, and mind-boggling." Marcia points out that "maleness" and "femaleness" are also part of each individual, just as both aspects are part of God. "It is exciting to support the feminine dimension within my spouse through my being, as he supports the masculine dimension in me through his being. In this relationship, I feel partnered in a complete and fulfilling way. Perhaps this is why in the Torah, we hear God calling us as individuals not to be alone, but to be in partnership."

Rabbi Marcia points out, however, that holy partnering is not exclusive to heterosexual relationships: "Jewish tradition teaches that *Kedusha*, holiness, is found within marriage, but in a growing sector of the Jewish community there is increasing acknowledgment that the sacred can be expressed in all committed, loving relationships, including same-sex unions."

Rabbi Marcia's description blends religious and psychological understandings of marriage. The sacredness of human partnership is emphasized by comparing the marriage of two people with the marriage between God and God's people. By wrestling with each other, the couple experiences God-wrestling as well. By locating and honoring each one's feminine and masculine aspects, they more fully reflect the feminine and masculine aspects of the Divine, individually and as a couple.

The wrestling image also illustrates Swiss psychologist Carl Jung's description of marriage as a psychological relationship. Jung asserted that by struggling with each other, two people could discover unconscious aspects of themselves. By integrating their shadow sides and the feminine and masculine energies within each of them, each person could become more conscious, more in touch with their true self. While Jung believed this type of growth was the goal of a mature relationship, he acknowledged that most marriages never reached it, focusing instead on the preservation of the species.

With the consumer view of love, we marry for what we'll get out of it. We may even see psychological growth as something that is for our own benefit, or the mutual benefit of both partners. But when marriage is seen as a spiritual path, it transcends the two people involved. We are not just wrestling each other; we are also wrestling the Divine. Roman Catholics describe marriage as a sacrament to convey that the sacred is present in the joining of two partners. Marriage is a channel of grace, a way of experiencing God's love. In *Called: New Thinking on Christian Vocation*, Roman

Catholic monk M. Basil Pennington writes, "The human heart wants an infinite love. If the marriage partners seek this in each other they are bound to be disappointed and frustrated." Only if they help each other seek God's love, "then their aspiration for infinite love can be fulfilled and in that love their mutual love can be limitless." In this understanding, growth through marriage is a way for two people to experience God.

Many cultures have seen the sexual aspect of marriage as a special experience of transcendence. In Tantric Yoga, sexual pleasure is said to release *kundalini,* the sacred energy which enables lovers to feel one with the Divine. In Taoism, sex is seen as a way to balance yin and yang, the feminine and masculine energies of the universe, and Taoist men are taught that giving their female partners pleasure is itself a spiritual practice. Although the Judeo-Christian tradition has emphasized the procreative potential of sex—with Christian churches often portraying sex as an obstacle to spiritual growth—both Judaism and Christianity have also taught that sex can be an expression of holiness, uniting physical and spiritual experience.

What all these perspectives have in common is the belief that sexual relationship is a path, not a destination; it is an expression of love and holiness, not a god in and of itself. This view need not devalue the strength of desire, the joy of pleasure, the human need for sexual bonding. Seeing the sacred dimension of sex actually gives it more value than the books and magazine articles that focus exclusively on technique, as if mastering a new sexual skill will make sex meaningful. Unlike the technical approaches that separate sex from soul, most spiritual traditions teach that sex reaches its sacred potential in the context of an ongoing relationship where partners give their whole selves to each other, not just their bodies.

Although the major religions have generally defined such relationships as heterosexual, there is now a small but growing segment of the religious world that also recognizes gay partnership as a potential path to transcendence. This comes from the recognition that God calls people to different forms of loving. For some, heterosexual marriage is the spiritual path that will help them grow toward God. For others, gay partnership is such a path. Still others feel called to a life of singleness or even solitude. To love most fully, it is important that we discover the form of loving meant for us.

The process of discovering our path is itself full of opportunities for spiritual growth. We may come to know ourselves more deeply. We may strengthen our relationship to the Divine. We may learn trust and patience though periods of uncertainty. These experiences will become the bricks upon which any future marriage is built. Those who hope to find a partner may feel frustrated as they wait for the right person to appear or for that person to commit. They may feel they can't begin the journey until someone else joins them. But the path of committed relationship begins with our approach toward singleness and dating. Rejecting the consumer approach to love and learning to trust in love's abundance will lead to a different type of relationship than desperate, manipulative dating tactics.

THE PATH BEFORE PARTNERSHIP

Late one night when I was in graduate school, my friend Tracy and I sat in my room, our minds exhausted from lofty intellectual pursuits, tittering about the men in our departments. Sprawled across my floor, we each took a piece of paper and wrote out the ten most important qualities we were looking for in a man. I was amazed by how specific Tracy was, down to the preferred lip thickness of her ideal partner. My qualities were much more esoteric. Sympathy with oppressed people was high on my list. So was sense of humor.

I now believe that having a shopping list keeps us from seeing others, no matter what qualities are on our inventory. Several years ago, I began dating Alix, and during our first lunch together, we each indicated we were potentially in the market for marriage and children. We spent the rest of our eight-month relationship running down our shopping lists, checking off required qualities as we found them. Physically attractive, check. Good sense of humor, check. Sympathy with oppressed people, oops! Only after several months did I realize how different our values were. In retrospect, I don't believe I ever knew this man. I was so busy weighing his assets and debits I never stopped to listen to who he really was.

After my relationship with Alix, I realized I wanted to do things differently in the future. First, I revised my checklist; then gave up the list altogether. I began to trust that I would be given all I needed, even if it wasn't in the form I had wanted or expected. I even began to let go of the idea of looking for a partner, trusting that if I was meant to marry, it would happen when the time was right.

Thirty-seven-year-old Betsy has had a similar experience. A professional teacher whose colorful apartment is full of books and dried flowers, Betsy explains how studying *A Course in Miracles* has changed her perspective on looking for someone to marry. "I sincerely believe that if God intends me to have a husband—whatever God is, that numinous unknown which to me is sometimes as real as the cup I'm holding—then that person will come into my life." Betsy says often a person she really needed to learn from has appeared in her life at just the right moment. "I've had many situations where this has happened, so why not in love too?" she asks. Learning to trust that she'll meet a partner if she is meant to has brought more peace into Betsy's life. "It may or may not happen," she says, "so I really don't worry about it. I've just let that go, and I'm quite calm about it."

Reaching this attitude of calm—what Buddhists call nonattachment—is not always easy. Loneliness, social pressure, and the desire for children can all add to our anxiety about singleness. Yet these factors also offer opportunities to face our fears and come to know ourselves more deeply. For me, a period of being single and hoping for partnership helped me to learn patience. I learned to let go of my agenda and trust in love's abundance. While waiting, I focused on deepening my relationship with God, spending more time in quiet than I would have had I been with a man. Not only did this period of spiritual growth lay the foundation for my marriage, it helped me to learn important lessons that enrich other aspects of my life as well.

Seeking the sacred dimension of romantic love changes our whole approach to relationships. Fiona, a dynamic Englishwoman in her twenties, is animated as she explains how her recent spiritual awakening has changed what she is looking for in a partner. "Their spiritual self would now be a lot more important to me," states Fiona. "I can't say, 'Tom Hanks is my ideal man. I wish I could meet somebody like him.' Neither can I say, 'Well, I'd like A, B, C qualities in my perfect person.' I'm much more willing to wait and see what comes my way and then work out if that's right."

Just as waiting offers many lessons, working out if a relationship is right for us also presents opportunities for spiritual growth. Choosing a partner may help us learn spiritual discernment—the practice of listening within for divine guidance (discussed in the next chapter). Instead of consulting our shopping list, we consult our hearts to see if a relationship brings a sense of peace and rightness. Choosing a partner may also force us to see ourselves more clearly, giving us unique insight into our beliefs and values. "My major relationships have been very influential in my spiritual formation," reflects Helen. Before she married, Helen seriously dated several men whose religious backgrounds were different from her own Lutheran upbringing. These relationships challenged Helen to explore her faith more deeply, spurring her search for a church that fit her beliefs more closely than Lutheranism.

Now a teacher and writer on contemporary mysticism, Renee first questioned the teachings of her Roman Catholic church while dating a Jewish man in college. Although her boyfriend thought the church's prohibition on premarital sex was foolish, Renee adhered to it for over a year. When their relationship ended almost two years later, Renee was devastated. "When Evan broke up with me," she recalls, "I realized I had substituted Evan, or my relationship with him, for God. When that relationship wasn't there, then the question 'Is there a God?' suddenly became very, very important again." Renee notes that questioning church teachings and learning to trust her own direct experiences of God were crucial steps in her spiritual development.

Romantic relationships, their giddy beginnings and painful endings, can force us to confront difficult but profound questions: Who am I? What is the purpose of my life? Is there a God who cares about me? Experiencing ourselves in relation to others may give us new insights into the answers to such questions. Dating need not be just a method for finding and selecting a spouse; it can also be a way to learn about ourselves and the art of loving.

Although making a commitment to one other person offers unique opportunities for growth, we may discover that our growth is fostered by some other way of life. Any form of love that extends us, that demands that we grow, that pushes us out of our selfishness can tap us into the source. We do not need a partner to begin the work of loving. Although discerning a call to marriage is the focus of this book, marriage is not the only way people are called to love. Ultimately my concern is not with finding a partner but finding the path that will unleash the great love within us.

CHAPTER TWO

Growing as a Lover

*E*very month as I file through the supermarket checkout line, I notice a new magazine headline inquiring about my romantic future. "Will Your Love Last?" wonders *Glamour*. "Is This the Man You Want to Marry?" asks *Cosmopolitan*. A multiple-choice quiz and simple score chart give us the answer: 95–140 points, Marrying Man; 45–90 points, Mr. Maybe; 0–40 points, Dumping Material.

I suspect most women take these quizzes only half seriously, but their popularity reveals a hunger for guidance in matters of the heart. Some part of us wants to be told how we should live and whom we should love. Taking the latest quiz or reading the latest book (including this one!) is easier than standing alone with our questions. I know there have been times when I've wished for clear instructions, even a numerical score rating a relationship's potential. Gradually I've learned that instead of outside authorities (whether girlfriends or self-help authors), my own inner voice is the best source of romantic guidance. This voice, which some call the God-within, always knows whether or not a relationship is right for me.

Listening to the source of wisdom within us points us in a different direction than the cost-benefit analyses of popular dating strategies. The spiritual and psychological process of discovering our true selves can help us to hear our inner voice and find the way of life that will enable us to express our love most fully, whether through celibacy, parenthood, heterosexual or same-gender partnership, or some other lifestyle.

"Are You Meant to Be Married?" asks *Complete Woman* magazine. Listen: The answer lies within you.

SPIRITUAL DISCERNMENT

Pat, a warm and creative woman with colorful dangling earrings and a silver ponytail, laughs heartily as she recalls her mother saying, "Oh honey, when you meet the right one, you'll *know!*" Pat says, "We laugh about it, but I think it holds true. You just know that you know." She notes that in today's culture people are reluctant to trust this knowing. "We're such mind thinkers that we don't allow for this other space," she says, pointing to her abdomen. A devout Presbyterian, Pat explains that this inner mysterious space is where she connects to God and feels God's guidance. When her inner guide led her to marry Tom, a Presbyterian minister, and move with him to work in a drug-infested urban neighborhood, Pat was initially terrified, but in prayer she felt reassured that it was the right thing to do. Now with several years hindsight, Pat remains confident that God led her to this man and his ministry.

The belief that we can hear God's guidance if we wait

and listen for it is common to the two religious traditions that have influenced me the most: Catholicism, the faith I grew up with, and Quakerism, which I embraced as an adult. Roman Catholics have a wealth of literature on listening to God—from the writings of Saint Ignatius to modern guides on vocational discernment—and an abundance of retreat houses for this purpose. The belief that God speaks to us directly is the root of Quakerism and the reason silence is central to Quaker worship. By waiting and listening in silence, we invite the Spirit to guide us in our individual and collective actions.

Discernment is the process of discovering how we are called to act, in everyday decisions as well as in major life choices. Some define it as listening for God's guidance, while others think of it as following their deepest, truest self. The term *inner voice* describes the root of wisdom within us, and people of many faiths believe that God speaks through this voice. Those who don't use God-language may still experience a deep sense of knowing or direction. One friend of mine calls it discovering "the Truth of a situation." I understand discernment as the process of connecting to the divine source and letting myself be guided by it, though I am less interested in honing a definition of discernment than in honoring the experience.

In the course of my interviews, people used different words to describe this process, but at the same time, there were striking similarities. Many found that a sense of peace or deep *knowing* came to them, often when they least expected it. Several said that too much thinking made it harder to reach clarity. Waiting and patiently listening within for an answer were usually important, along with a feeling of openness to what would come. For some, being open required letting go of conformity and the desire to please family and friends. For others, being open meant letting go of their own agendas and surrendering to the unexpected. Like Pat, many found that when they trusted their inner guide and took a risk, their faith in the mysterious space was confirmed and strengthened.

Renee, a thirty-six-year-old writer and teacher on mystical experience, observes, "Relationship issues—who to get involved with, whether or not to have sex with someone, whether or not to get married—were the issues in my life which were used to teach me discernment. Those were crucial decisions which I knew I couldn't make just with logic and analysis, as I had been taught. They had to be decisions of the heart as well, so I started paying attention to my feelings and intuition."

As a college freshman, Renee had to choose which of two suitors would become her first boyfriend. Although she liked both men, she was hit by a strong intuition that she should choose Evan rather than Toby. Renee and Toby were very similar and Renee felt a strong soul connection with him. "I had this strange feeling that somehow Toby would be part of my whole life," she recalls. "But Evan, who was very different from me in a lot of ways, was someone I only had this one opportunity to get to know, and therefore I should get involved with Evan. This thought came to me with certainty and a feeling of rightness," says Renee. "Then I didn't have any difficulty making the choice, although I felt bad Toby was hurt."

In hindsight Renee believes her intuition was correct. Toby has remained a lifelong friend, while her relationship with Evan—whose personality and religious background were both very different from hers—taught Renee a great deal about herself and other people. Over the years, Renee has come to trust her intuition as a source of sacred guidance. Sometimes, when she is attracted to a man her intuition tells her would not be good for her, Renee may initially resist her inner guide, but she has learned to always follow it.

I learned to trust internal cues long before I learned the word *discernment* or associated it with God. When I was a college senior, I spent months anguishing over career options, boiling them down to two diverging possibilities: becoming an investment banker on Wall Street or joining the Peace Corps. After several bank interviews, I began to notice my own reactions. Although I always read news about Africa or Asia, I found the paper's business section more boring than my economics classes. I fantasized about learning Swahili or Arabic, whereas the thought of sitting behind a polished Manhattan desk made my throat constrict. I couldn't breathe in pin stripes. I couldn't think in high heels. When I threw out the assumption that salary was the most important criteria and simply listened to my heart, it was clear I was not meant to be an investment banker. I *knew* joining the Peace Corps was the right thing to do.

Many of my Duke classmates, on the other hand, made career decisions without consulting their hearts or souls. When I asked one wealthy senior what he planned to do after graduation, he said, "My father wants me to go to law school, and my mother wants me to go to business school. I think I'll go to business school because I like my mom better." Knowing he had a huge trust fund and an almost straight A average, I was shocked that he perceived so few possibilities for himself. I prodded him to say what *he* wanted, but he dismissed the question. Finally I framed it as fantasy: "If you had a magic year that no one else had to know about where you could do anything you wanted . . ." He leaned over and confided in a whisper, "I've always wanted to be a third-grade teacher." When I said he would be a wonderful teacher, his guard shot back up. "No," he concluded, "my family would never accept that." I heard a year later that, like his father, he had gone to law school.

In choosing to become a lawyer, this man chose to center his life around someone else's ambitions. As a result, he missed an opportunity for growth, in himself and in his relationship with his father. Asserting his own aspirations would have been difficult, but it might have led to more honest communication and more genuine loving within his family. Whether or not he was actually called to teach, simply by denying the possibility he precluded a chance to become more fully himself.

Distinguishing a desire from a calling can be difficult, but to begin the process we must acknowledge our desires rather than repress them. If we simply conform to someone else's plan for us in exchange for the illusion of acceptance and security, we will never find our true path. This doesn't mean becoming individualistic, rebelling against family or community for the thrill of being different. Discernment means searching for the truth of a situation, tapping into the source, desiring the greatest good. Whether we think of it as seeking God's will, getting in rhythm with the universe, or finding our cosmic niche, discernment does require believing in a Truth that is bigger than what we want right now. We are not just listening to our hearts; we are listening *with* our hearts to something greater than ourselves.

Historically, the term *discernment* is shorthand for "discernment of spirits," an acknowledgment that not all the voices we hear are of God. As we listen within, we may hear competing voices, including insecurities, repressed emotions, and social pressures we have internalized. We may need to patiently allow our fears and resistances to rise to the surface before we can distinguish them from the deep, true voice. This process of distinguishing is the essence of discernment, which comes from the Latin word *discernere*, "to separate by sifting."

There are various approaches to this sifting, from the structured, intellectual method of Saint Ignatius of Loyola to the more intuitive, community-based approach used by many Quakers. Most spiritual traditions, recognizing the temptation to hear what we want to hear and call it God's will, offer some signposts for discerning a call. Many Christians refer to the "fruits of the Spirit" listed in Paul's letter to the Galatians: "love, joy, peace, patience, kindness, goodness, trustfulness, gentleness, and self-control." We are not meant to look for these fruits only in our major life decisions but in all our actions. In fact, it is by cultivating our ongoing connection to the Spirit that we best cultivate discernment and its fruits. As Taoism teaches, "If you want the proper results you must learn the Great Way," then you will realize "great fruits."

Kathryn, a seminary graduate in her mid-forties, teaches a Quaker approach to inward listening. "I think there's been a distortion about discernment," reflects Kathryn, who feels called to a life of celibacy and solitude. "We often think that major life decisions are the most important aspects of discernment, like whether you get married or whether you don't. But it's actually those little discernments every day that shape us into the person we are." When asked how she made the choice to live a single, celibate life, Kathryn responds, "I have trouble even with the idea of making a choice. It's more like listening to what God is calling forth already, to see how God has worked in your life, to see how healing is being called for. I think we're dipping into a stream that is already flowing." The real choice, says Kathryn, is to listen to the patterns of our experience. By paying attention to her persistent need for solitude and her desire to be alone with God, Kathryn came to recognize her calling to singleness.

Ongoing spiritual practices can help us listen to the patterns of our experience—such as prayer, meditation, journal writing, or scripture reading. Being part of a spiritual community can also be important grounding, especially when we allow people we trust to give us feedback on the fruits of our discernment. In Quaker practice, for example, we can ask for a "clearness committee," a small group of discerners who through deep listening and supportive questioning help us sort through an issue or decision we are facing. *Listening Hearts: Discerning Call in Community*, a book that synthesizes major schools of discernment, offers suggestions for how people can support each other's discernment. As the authors note, "Discernment is a gift from God. But it also includes an intentional attempt on our part to hear God's call in our life. It takes work; it is also a matter of grace."

We may feel God's grace most dramatically when after difficult indecision we feel a sudden sense of peace or clarity. We stop churning an issue over in our minds because we *know* what we must do. We may not have the practical details worked out—in fact, our call may not seem practical at all—but still we feel a sense of rightness about it. One way to confirm this sense is to see if it lasts over time, especially through ups and downs. If the peace lasts, it may be a sign that we have heard our call correctly.

Sandra compares discernment to giving birth. "You go through all this pain and turmoil and deep breathing, and finally this thing, this decision, comes out. If it's the right decision," she notes, "I feel at peace." Sandra, a Costa Rican artist in her mid-twenties who lives and works at a spiritual study center in the United States, recalls her recent struggle over whether or not to end a seven-month-long romantic relationship. Talking through her doubts with a trusted friend helped her see that this relationship did not have the long-term potential Sandra had wanted. But it was during silent community meditation that Sandra finally felt peace and clarity about what she needed to do. "It was just clear," she says. Even though the breakup was difficult, Sandra says she felt at peace throughout, a confirmation to her that ending the relationship was the right decision.

Although peace and love are hallmarks of discernment, our guidance may not necessarily be comfortable for ourselves or those around us. Many who are viewed as prophets or saints today felt called to challenge the norms of their times, often evoking scorn and persecution. If we dare to ask the question "How is God calling me to live?" we have to face the possibility that we will be led in directions which seem peculiar, or even threatening, to those around us. One challenging aspect of discernment is putting our desire to do what is right ahead of our desire to be understood and accepted.

This is shown in the life of Joan of Arc, who at sixteen defied her parents and refused to marry, obeying instead the voices she heard which directed her to lead the French in resisting English occupation. Although Joan believed these voices were holy, she sometimes resisted their advice out of fear. At one point, to avoid death at the stake, Joan disobeyed her voices and signed an oath recanting her previous statements of faith. But the voices urged her to be true to her call, and within days she rescinded the oath and faced death by fire. Although most of us feel called to less dramatic acts, we may be just as frightened of their repercussions. We may resist a calling before we accept it, as Joan did. Or we may repress our inner voice rather than risk rejection by those close to us, as did the young man who was afraid to acknowledge his desire to teach because it would bring conflict with his family.

The young man most likely used logic to justify his decision, recounting the persuasive arguments of his lawyer father. Although logic could not explain or soothe the yearning to teach, the young man had been trained to trust rational thinking over intuition. Nothing in his education or upbringing had taught him to listen to that part of himself that had always wanted to be a third-grade teacher. Given the more lucrative and prestigious options available to him, teaching was not a logical choice and therefore was discounted. This same faith in analytical thinking is evident in the mating guides that urge us to get a logical grip on our relationships and learn the "skill" of evaluating a potential spouse. We are told to conduct a cost-benefit analysis of the marriage we are considering without ever asking ourselves how we are called to act.

After two disastrous marriages, Carolyn says that listening to her head rather than her heart brought her a lot of misery. "When God has a purpose in your life, He won't let you have no peace until that purpose is fulfilled," says Carolyn, who returned to the Pentecostal church of her youth several years ago. Now forty-two and expecting her fifth grandchild, Carolyn explains that for the many years she was away from the church she did what seemed easy or convenient rather than seeking the Lord's guidance. For example, both times she married she knew deep down that it was a mistake. "Before I married my last husband, I could hear a little voice in me always saying he wasn't for me. I just ignored it and went on and married him anyway, even though I knew it was wrong. And there was a lot of suffering, a lot of needless pain. I guess I was looking for security," she explains. "This man seemed like the perfect man. He seemed like he loved me dearly. He loved my children. He was a good provider. But he had his hidden secrets too." Describing the twelve years of their marriage—including his drinking, his temper, and his adultery—Carolyn notes that she would have been better off listening to the little voice inside her that she believes comes from God. Rather than seeking security in a man, she now trusts that God will provide for her and let her know when she is headed in the right direction.

Carolyn was not listening for guidance when she decided to marry. In fact, she deliberately pushed aside the warning she was hearing. But what if we are trying to listen, and we are still unsure of what to do? Asking how we are called may seem overwhelming, frightening, or impossible to answer. Indeed it is wise to approach this question with humility, recognizing that we may never be certain we have heard our call correctly. Yet neither should we let the hugeness of the question paralyze us. In *Called: New Thinking on Christian Vocation*, Roman Catholic monk and writer M. Basil Pennington recalls his struggle as a young man trying to discern his life's direction and his fear that there was "one slot for me and it was all-important for me to find it and live in it. A failure to discover it or persevere in it and all would be lost." Pennington argues that such anxiety does not facilitate discernment. Instead of worrying so much about our life decisions, Pennington suggests we simply ask, "Which way can I best grow as a lover?"

This question stands in stark contrast to those we usually ask: Which job pays the most? Which way of life gives me the most comfort/prestige/security? Which guy is the best deal? When we change our focus from what we will receive to what we will become, a different set of priorities emerge, along with a different way of deciding. We put aside our shopping list and search instead for internal guides. The question "Which way can I best grow as a lover?" cannot be answered by logic alone. That answer must emerge from our hearts, based on knowledge about ourselves as much as knowledge about the options we are considering.

DISCOVERING OUR TRUE SELVES

The difference between Cheryl's decision to marry the first time, at age twenty-two, and her decision to marry the second time, at age thirty-one, illustrates the importance of self-knowledge. Reflecting on the failure of her first marriage, Cheryl states, "I thought that somehow a man could make me be something I was not. I married someone who was very different from me, who came from a Southern Baptist family as opposed to northeastern Jewish." His parents, who were both civil rights activists, seemed very romantic compared with Cheryl's own suburban family. "I felt like marrying into that would make me a different person," she says.

In retrospect, Cheryl realizes she did not yet know who she was in her own right. "Finding who you are, and how you're going to carve out your niche and where is a very tricky thing to balance for two lives. It's much easier if you meet a person once you both know who you are. In years past, women just followed men's paths, and now there's a whole other dimension that has to be factored in." Cheryl says of her first marriage, "We definitely started out with him being the senior member of the partnership and me the junior, and as that changed, it was harder for him than it was for me. The second time I got married was very different because then I was established as a professional person. I knew who I was and what my strengths were. I no longer needed a man to make me who I wasn't. So I entered into my second marriage as an equal, as opposed to a subservient, and that's really important."

When she met William, Cheryl was impressed that, unlike her first husband, he was not threatened by her professional success. "He celebrated my success and was actually attracted to me because of what I did and the fact that I was an independent person. And yet, he was also very nurturing and supportive." Cheryl recalls, "For me what was striking about William was that I always felt safe—safe in being myself around him, not that I had to be someone different, and somehow safer in the world with this person." Several other people interviewed made similar comments, saying that when they met their spouse they knew it was "right" because they felt comfortable being themselves.

Discovering our true selves is an important theme in both religion and psychology. For Swiss psychologist Carl Jung, this painful process was the purpose of human life, serving the greater collective good rather than the individual's success in worldly terms. Discovering our true selves was also an important theme for Thomas Merton, a Trappist monk whose voluminous writings on the spiritual life are widely respected. Whereas Jung flirted with religious language, Merton described self-discovery in explicitly religious terms, insisting that it was "by the door of this deep self that we enter into the spiritual knowledge of God."

Discovering our true selves requires us to strip away the masks we wear every day—the false images we project, even our ideas about what we should think and feel—to discover a more authentic person, the person we were created to be.

Merton put this point strongly: "Before we can realize who we really are, we must become conscious of the fact that the person we think we are, here and now, is at best an impostor and a stranger." This is a challenging statement, and one most of us would rather ignore. To recognize the many ways in which we pretend to be what we're not can be frightening and painful, but it is essential if we are to recognize our manipulative tendencies and begin to move past them.

When Renee was choosing her first boyfriend, her intuition told her she would learn a lot from a relationship with Evan. She didn't realize she would learn just as much from their breakup three years later. "It was an intense, emotionally shattering experience, an incredibly painful rejection," she states, "but I think that pain and what it opened me up to was a crucial stage in my spiritual development." Renee explains, "I was feeling emotions I had never felt before that I didn't know I was capable of, like jealousy, and the desire to beg him to come back, which was kind of degrading since he wasn't interested in me." Renee felt she had a choice: she could either accept these feelings as part of herself or she could deny them by blaming her ex-boyfriend. Blaming would protect her from some of the pain of rejection, "but I wouldn't be in touch anymore with who I really was," she explains. "When I began to accept my painful emotions, I had an image of making myself sit there and feel my feelings, moving back into the center of my body, especially my heart, and into my true self. Feeling these horrible things was part of my true self even though I didn't like it. I think because I learned to do that, I'm more in touch with my intuition than most people are." Renee, who believes we can feel God's guidance through intuition and dreams, states, "There are so many times over the course of one's life when there are opportunities to be your true self or your false self.

When being your true self is really painful, we tend to block those things off, and when we do we also block off a lot of our intuition."

As Renee points out, being her true self did not mean taking her pain out on her ex-boyfriend; it meant feeling the hurt herself. It meant giving up her image of herself as someone who was above jealousy and desperation. Jung said giving up false self-images was essential to becoming conscious; Merton said it was essential for knowing God. Again and again Merton stressed that true self-discovery does not mean defining ourselves by what makes us different or separate—quite the opposite. Giving up our false self enables us to feel one with other people and with God. Our true identity, Merton said, is always rooted in God.

Both Jung and Merton saw self-discovery as a lifelong process, a thought I find comforting at moments when I realize how much I have yet to learn. Although I now cry and express anger more easily than I did ten years ago, I know I have yet to fully face my shadow and still resist doing so. My marriage helps chip away at this resistance through the everyday struggles of living with another person. Though it is sometimes tempting to bury difficult emotions in the name of keeping the peace, I know Tom is the right partner for me because in the end I always feel safe showing him the parts of myself I would rather hide.

Dating and choosing a life partner present many opportunities for authenticity or deception. I recall one relationship where I deliberately wore more makeup than usual because I knew my boyfriend liked it. My motivation wasn't to please him but to win his approval. In other subtle ways I was not myself. When in his car, I bit my tongue at the angry, impatient gestures he made at other drivers, not wanting to start an argument over behavior I found disturbing. I hid the crisis I was facing at work, not wanting him to know my own angry, impatient side. Ultimately, that was how I knew it was not the right relationship; I didn't feel honest with him. Although I had spent a lot of energy evaluating "Who is he?" in the end I realized the more important question was "Who am I when I'm with him?"

After going to college in different states, twenty-four-year-old Jodi and her high school sweetheart, Bruce, have resumed their relationship. He is planning to move to Jodi's city in a few weeks, and she can barely contain her excitement as she talks about him. "One of the reasons Bruce and I get along so well is that I can be myself with him," she explains. "I can say all my quirky thoughts, and he understands them." Because Jodi is herself with Bruce, he is able to help her sort through career decisions by honestly observing her strengths and weaknesses. This helps her to see herself more clearly and makes her feel loved for who she really is.

Recalling the college years when she and Bruce dated other people, Jodi says, "I've gone out with a lot of guys where I felt like I was putting on a show until I got to know them better, but then it never quite got to that point." Jodi remembers thinking, "I have to wear my hair this way or say the right things or maybe he's not going to like me." In one relationship, she acted more socially conscious than she really was to win the approval of the doctoral student she was dating. Jodi says that when pretending in a relationship, "You just feel awful."

With the consumer approach to dating, we may try a little false advertising, changing our appearance or behavior to give the customer what we think he wants. But this strategy is unloving and misguided. Burying our true selves in order to catch or keep a partner makes real intimacy impossible. We never feel loved and accepted for who we really are. Whatever connection develops is only as deep as our makeup.

A lot of popular dating advice focuses on how we can change our appearance, from how to "fake a great beach body" to hiding gray hair and wrinkles. The fear that our bodies must be disguised, thinned, made over, or otherwise altered in order to be attractive is particularly common among women. This fear damages our self-awareness as well as our self-esteem. Instead of knowing ourselves by our thoughts and feelings, the inner experiences that make us truly unique, too often we know ourselves by our dress size or hair color. Instead of joyously accepting our sexual feelings, we compare ourselves to airbrushed magazine covers and feel ashamed. We may lunge desperately at any man who comes along. Or we may stifle our desires for fear of being rejected. In either case, unconscious insecurity about our bodies limits our ability to love.

Once we befriend them, our bodies can be instruments of discernment, offering us important information and insights. The pit of our stomachs or the hair on the back of our necks can warn us when something isn't right. A feeling of deep relaxation or renewed energy may signal inner peace. Sayings such as "My blood boiled" and "My heart skipped a beat" describe how these emotions register physically. When we are excessively busy or disconnected from our bodies, we may miss the signals they are sending. Renee's image of moving back into the center of her body shows how the integration of our emotional and physical lives helps us be more authentic.

My body often forces me to deal with emotions I would rather deny. When I am under pressure, a sore throat and stuffy nose compel me to admit my anxiety. Sometimes I don't realize I am sad until I feel my tear ducts start to fill. Premenstrual syndrome, in particular, has often forced me to acknowledge difficult emotions, like anger, and sadness. In my experience, hormonal changes do not create emotions in me; they simply lower my defense mechanisms, making it harder for me to hide my real feelings and, as a result, helping me see a situation more honestly. Listening to our bodies can also be important in discerning our feelings toward another person. Flushed cheeks or a quickened heartbeat can alert us to our sexual feelings, whereas a lack of attraction to a date or a partner can prompt us to examine how we're feeling about the relationship. Acknowledging our emotions to ourselves not only helps us to know ourselves more deeply, it also helps in the sifting of discernment.

We have an amazing capacity to hide our true feelings from ourselves, though not without consequences. For example, Jane was married for twenty-five years and raised three children before she realized she was a lesbian. "Coming out to myself opened a whole area inside me that had been closed," explains Jane. "It was that which precipitated the end of my marriage." Fran, even after four children and twenty years of marriage, did not realize she was a lesbian until seven years after her divorce. Now in a committed partnership with each other, Jane and Fran realize how much of themselves they had repressed in order to function in a heterosexual culture. Jane, who has recently become a professional quilter, compares it to living all your life in black and white and then one day discovering color. Along with her sexual awakening came an explosion of creativity and a new awareness of her spirituality. "It's not just about sex," explains Fran, a professional therapist. "It's about knowing who we are." She states that they both feel much more alive spiritually since coming out of the closet. "Because I know who I am now, I have a me to offer God," says Fran.

Fran's statement illustrates Merton's point about stripping away false selves. While pretending to be a happy heterosexual, Fran was alienated from her true self and, as a result, felt separate from God and other human beings. Although coming out was a crucial step in her growth, she continues to learn who she is through her relationship with Jane. Fran explains, "When you make yourself vulnerable to another person, letting them know what is going on inside of you, then they can reflect back to you. So you get clearer about who you are. I can see myself more clearly because Jane can shine a light on my blind spots."

Through their relationship, Jane and Fran have more to offer each other and the world around them. They share a depth of trust that neither felt in her marriage, and they consciously foster each other's creative talents. Fran states, "We want to encourage the growth of each of us and become more who we are through our relationship." This includes nurturing each woman's individual relationship with the Divine as well as their connection with each other.

FORMS OF LOVING

The primary form our loving takes is very personal. Some individuals are meant to express their love in partnership, others in a single life committed to service. Some discover their capacity to love through parenthood, whereas others have their hearts opened in solitude. Some are called to love members of their own sex. Still others find ways of loving that defy traditional categories. For this reason, social norms that declare "everyone should live this way" can pull us away from our intended path, making it harder for us to be loving. God calls us to learn who we are so we can find the way of life that allows us to love most fully.

The term *vocation* comes from the Latin word *vocare*, "to call," and in the religious sense, it means a calling from God. It may be our work—painting, healing, building houses—or our lifestyle—singleness, partnership, monastic life, etc. Commitment over time is part of what distinguishes a vocation from what Quakers call a "leading." For example, we may feel led to donate food for people who were recently flooded out of their homes, but that leading does not imply a continued future obligation. If we repeatedly feel called to aid in disaster relief, however, we may discern a vocation to this type of work. We may receive Red Cross training and promise to show up whenever our services are needed. This type of vocation includes commitment without any specified time frame or vows. Other vocations, like marriage or vowed religious life, include specific promises, traditionally including a lifelong commitment.

Vocation is not a single action. As one woman I interviewed observed, "God might call you to do little specific things every day, and vocation would be a major strand of these little calls." Conducting interviews for this book, I became increasingly convinced that vocation is the way of life that allows us to love most fully. Rather than the job or lifestyle that gives us the most, vocation is the way we give ourselves. If we are living a vocation, our total capacity to love is expanded.

A forty-year-old Franciscan sister and peace activist, Michelle says her vocation to celibacy frees her "to love as Jesus loved, which means all kinds of people, no matter what color the skin, whether they're female or male, whether they're poor or rich." She recalls recently sending an affirming note to a discouraged male coworker and says it is "safe" for her to show love "without a lot of other baggage being read into it." Michelle adds that celibacy and support from her community of sisters enable her to do challenging work for peace and social justice that she might not attempt if she had a spouse or children. Kathryn, the Quaker discernment teacher who also feels called to celibacy, says marriage is like a spotlight where you focus your love on one person, whereas celibacy is like a floodlight, allowing love to be spread more broadly.

Both Michelle and Kathryn feel expanded by their lifestyle, not limited. This is very different from someone who is forced to be celibate against the deeper yearnings of their heart. Imposed celibacy can cause one to become bitter and cut off from others, eclipsing one's love rather than spreading it. A true calling to celibacy, like any vocation, can enable one to love more fully.

"If you are in a vocation, that is where God wants you to be," states Rebecca softly and clearly. "There may be sacrifice, but there's not martyrdom." Rebecca's quiet presence reflects the depth of her Christian faith and her choice to center her life on God, foregoing television, movies, and other forms of mainstream culture. Rebecca's primary vocation is motherhood, and for her this means making decisions according to what is best for her family as a whole, even when it conflicts with her individual ambitions and desires. As a single working mother, the sacrifices are many. Rebecca admits the difficulty and adds, "I can feel the moments when I'm being met by something that I can't quite find words for, where a love just overflows, and I *want* to make the sacrifice."

Wanting to give oneself fully, even through sacrifice or

struggle, is typical of those living a vocation. In fact, many women I spoke to said it was the challenge of their way of life that brought them the most growth. For example, the loneliness and isolation of celibacy helps Kathryn turn more fully to God. For some, the disagreements that arise in marriage teach compassion and forgiveness. For Rebecca, the challenge of being inclusive, considering her two children's needs along with her own, has helped her face her own selfish and manipulative side. This growth in self-awareness has enabled her to be more loving, not just with her children, but with others as well.

When struggling with the demands of motherhood, people have often asked Rebecca, "Well, what have you done for yourself lately?" She recalls bristling at the question. "I would sometimes just hold my abdomen and let myself stay in touch with the stretch marks on my belly. These stretch marks signify a self that's different than the self they're speaking to. I am no longer isolated, able to choose what feels good just to me, which is how I heard the question. I have done something here that informs me of my deep connectedness. I'm interwoven and interconnected in many, many other ways as well, such that I now hear the question, and I want to answer back, 'What have you done for yourself lately that has yielded fruit for others?' I want to really trust the commandment to love God first and to love one's neighbor as oneself. That carries a wonderful mystery, and the promise is that there are choices that cut all ways."

Rebecca's insight that "there are choices that cut all ways" helped me understand another aspect of vocation. We are meant to love God, self, *and* others. These three need not be in competition. When we are living in the having mode, viewing love as a commodity in short supply, we assume there is only so much love to go around. We fear that loving God first means depriving ourselves. We imagine that loving ourselves makes us less loving toward others, or that loving another person keeps us from fully loving God. With a commodity concept of love, there is always scarcity. But if we see loving as an acknowledgment of our deep connectedness, to others and to God, we never need to ration love. Living a vocation means finding a way of life that allows us to love God, self, and others simultaneously.

This insight is particularly helpful today as traditional gender roles begin to loosen. Too often, women have been expected to serve God and others without honoring themselves. According to the market model, they have supplied love without demanding much of it. No wonder feminism seems threatening to those who see love as a scarce commodity. Women loving themselves, or each other, seems to limit the amount of love available for men and children, thus raising the price of love for everyone. Indeed, the danger is real. If women use their new freedoms to demand more for themselves without concern for others, they will only create an even more narcissistic, competitive society. This danger is epitomized by self-help manuals that claim to "empower" women by teaching them how to manipulate men.

This is where a spiritual approach to self-actualization differs from a secular self-help approach. Some self-help programs promote "self-awareness" and "self-esteem" as strategies to become more successful in love or business, teaching us how to get what we want without concern for others. Although it may be necessary for a woman who has never honored her own needs to focus on herself for a while, getting permanently stuck in selfishness does not help her reach wholeness. Putting the question "Which way can I best grow as a lover?" at the center of our self-exploration—

and keeping in mind that we don't mean lover only in the sexual sense—will help us distinguish loving self-care from self-centered individualism.

From this perspective, the changes brought by the modern women's movement can free us to find more fulfilling, expanding ways of loving. A woman who loves herself—who actively nourishes her own life and growth—will bear more fruit for others than one who is stifled, whether as a mother, a wife, a nun, or in any other role. If she can see herself as one strand of the complex web of creation—no more important than other strands, but also no less—she will begin to discover a richer way of loving, one that seeks the "choices that cut all ways." The challenge for men (as lovers, friends, fathers, or sons) is to love women through these changes, to foster women's life and growth, even when it seems to threaten men's security. Men will also benefit from less rigid gender roles, evidenced by the number of men now enriched by active parenting. As the patriarchal family disintegrates, we have the opportunity to replace it with richer, more varied, and more authentic ways of nurturing each other.

Learning to honor our own needs and those of a partner is central to the vocation of romantic partnership. Although sometimes frustrating, this challenge may teach us to love God, self, and others more fully. Patricia, who runs couples enrichment workshops with her husband, Brad, says, "You don't get married for better *or* for worse. You get married for better *and* for worse. There are simply bad times. There are times when he wants to zig and she wants to zag, and sometimes that's real easy to work out, and sometimes it's hard to work out." The potential of marriage, she asserts, is that if people can be flexible and creative and trust the changes that come with growth, then marriage can be a way for two people to support each other in their growth toward wholeness.

Annette believes she was called to the vocations of marriage and motherhood. Married to a Protestant minister for over thirty-four years, Annette notes that her greatest spiritual growth came through conflicts in her marriage. Now with four grown children, she reflects, "Love, compassion, faithfulness, and forgiveness are really what the Christian faith is about, and it seems to me that family is one of the most obvious ways to experience those things and practice them and live them out. In a certain sense, the hardest person to be compassionate with is the person you're closest to. It's easy to be more critical of your spouse than somebody else, because how somebody else acts doesn't reflect on you. Or your children, the people who are most closely identified with you. It's harder not to want to control what they do." The vocations of marriage and motherhood, Annette asserts, offer ample opportunities to learn to be more loving.

LISTENING FOR A CALL TO MARRIAGE

At the age of thirty, I began to give up my busyness and pay attention to my inner life. I left my job and became a resident student at Pendle Hill, a center for study and contemplation founded by Quakers. Every morning I joined people of many faiths for half an hour of worship rooted in silence, and over the course of several months I grew more comfortable with the insights that bubbled to the surface there. My inner growth was also nurtured by classes such as pottery, which reawakened dormant creativity, and a spiritual autobiography course, which helped me recognize patterns of my past. Washing dishes after lunch or singing for someone's birthday, I felt my connection to the community around me. Taking long walks in the nearby Swarthmore woods or weeding in the gardens, I felt my connection to all of creation.

During my second ten-week term at Pendle Hill, I felt connected in a different way as I became romantically involved with a new student named Kevin. Neighbors in the dorm, Kevin and I hit it off almost immediately, talking for hours about religion and job struggles. We had inside jokes that collapsed us in hysterics. We played duets on fiddle and guitar. But after two intense months, Kevin suddenly announced his need for distance. He said he didn't "feel centered" and "couldn't pray," reasons for breaking up I had never heard before. After a few weeks of painful discernment, Kevin decided to end the romantic aspect of our relationship while still remaining friends. I struggled to accept his boundary even though it was hard for me. At the same time, I struggled to accept my own needs and feelings. Instead of stifling my hurt and anger, as I had often done in the past, I expressed them. Kevin listened. As a result, I learned forgiveness, and Kevin and I developed a friendship much deeper than our initial romance.

Unconsciously, however, I still believed love was a scarce commodity, and this belief conflicted with my growing trust in divine guidance. Part of me was trying to "let go and let God," while another part of me confused letting go with playing hard to get, thinking that once I was no longer clinging, Kevin would realize how wonderful I was and come running back. This strategy worked to a degree, confusing us both. Eventually—through prayer, tears, and journal writing—I realized it was time to let go completely, to release us both from the ambiguous bond that left me feeling neither loved nor free.

It was near the end of this struggle that I discovered the courtship manuals and their shocking candor about their manipulative motives. The bare bones of wanting revealed in these books made me feel strangely vulnerable, as if my own protective skin might be stripped at any moment. Their manipulative strategies made me reflect on my own behavior in relationships and examine the motives behind it. I saw how I had been manipulative myself, in more subtle ways, and realized that I needed a whole new approach to relationships. I needed to discard my list of what I was looking for in a man. In fact, I needed to give up looking altogether. I decided to acknowledge to myself what I wanted—a committed partnership—and then wait, listening within to see if that desire came from my true self or my social conditioning. I decided I would only marry if I felt called to marriage as a vocation.

The call to marriage is hard, if not impossible, to discern in the abstract. Marriage is a commitment to another individual as much as it is to a married lifestyle. I wondered how I could hear this call, except in relation to a specific person who also felt called to marry me. Was the process of discerning this vocation even comparable to other alternatives? Being single and thirty-one, I wondered whether my growing attraction to partnership was a divine nudge or merely insecurity about becoming an old maid. How could I tell? And if I did feel called to partnership, what was I supposed to do in response? Submit my application the way one applies to law school?

I believe the principles of spiritual discernment apply to romantic decisions as they do to any others, though frankly I find discernment more difficult when it comes to romance, as if my inner compass gets pulled off course by the presence of a magnet. The tug of sexual attraction can be strong, and it is tempting to assume that such emotion must be divinely inspired. Add to this the strength of social conventions and the ticking of the biological clock, and we may find ourselves reeling. In a society where the assumptions about what women are supposed to want run so deep, how can we be sure we are listening to our true inner guide? How can we know whether our desires come from pressure or preference, culture or calling, backlash or biology? How can we know which way of life will help us to grow as a lover?

As Kathryn suggests, we can begin by listening to the patterns of our experience. This means carving time out of our busy schedules for quiet reflection and inner growth. It means paying attention to how we behave in romantic relationships, what our true feelings are, and how we deal with them. It means exploring our fears, whether fear of singleness or fear of commitment. And it means becoming aware of other forces that can pull us toward marriage, such as loneliness or the desire for children. Although anxiety can make discernment more difficult, identifying the pressures in our lives can help us distinguish the voices within us, making it easier (though not necessarily easy!) to know how we are meant to live.

CHAPTER THREE

Culture or Calling?
Backlash or Biology?

*C*ompeting with our inner voice are the voices of social pressure and insecurity. Since marriage is still the conventional choice, a woman who remains single may feel left out of the norm, awkward at dinner parties where guests come in twos, uncomfortable with inquiries about her single status. She may begin to tire of her friends' baby pictures and wonder if she'll ever have such photos herself. She may begin to glance in jewelry store windows and imagine the ring she would want to receive.

To determine whether such thoughts reflect an authentic desire to mate, we may need to sort through a pile of cultural baggage. It is often assumed that everyone wants to marry, and anyone who remains single is either concealing some ghastly flaw or suffering from "commitmentphobia." Such assumptions can raise insecurities, even among people who are confidently unconventional in other areas of their lives. Combined with loneliness and the biological clock, pressure to marry can make it hard to hear the voice of our true selves.

DOUBLE-EDGED ANXIETY

Kathryn says of her vocation to singleness, "There's nothing that affirms this lifestyle. I don't get any jubilees. Nobody's telling me, 'Right on honey, you've been faithful to your life for twenty-five years.' I don't get anniversaries like married people do. Sometimes I wish there was recognition for my commitment." She recalls once being invited to dinner by "very well meaning people" who lived on a nice farm. "And there was Ralph across from me. 'I'd like you to meet Ralph, the Tasty-cake salesman.'" Kathryn laughs, "I prefer an Entenmann's man, but I guess they figured, 'Honey, you're kind of old. You better settle for the Tasty-cake salesman.'"

Many single women report similar stories of friends trying to fix them up, even when the matchmaking is unwanted. As one thirty-eight-year-old single writer describes, "My *existence* makes people uncomfortable. I seem, perhaps, like one of those black socks you see lying by the side of the road, in the rain, without a mate." The writer, of course, is a woman.

I was recently at a party hosted by a good-looking, wealthy bachelor in his mid-forties. Throughout the evening, there were backslapping jokes about this being a wild bachelor's party. Men regarded him as a hero. Women described how they would redecorate his house if they had the chance. Afterward I tried to imagine how the atmosphere would have been different if the host had been female. Would people have called it a wild spinster's party? Would they have seen her single status as something to joke about, as if they were secretly envious?

Although men may also feel the weight of societal expectations, social pressure to marry is particularly strong for women, as Susan Faludi shows in her best-seller, *Backlash: The Undeclared War against American Women*. Through extensive research, Faludi documents how media images of single women changed from the seventies to the eighties, shifting from the cheerful Mary Tyler Moore to the crazed manhunter of *Fatal Attraction*. In reaction to rapidly changing gender roles, Faludi argues, there came a backlash against feminism. Sitcoms, movies, and magazines actively promoted marriage and motherhood as feminine ideals, along with the myth that "a woman over forty is more likely to be killed by a terrorist than to find a husband." Faludi shows how faulty statistics created a man-shortage myth that fueled single women's anxiety, making some "ready to marry men they didn't even love, just to beat the 'odds.' "

Faludi's work rightly demonstrates how a swing of the political pendulum can intensify social pressure on women to marry. But much as I respect Faludi's research, I felt frustrated as I finished *Backlash*, as if there was a missing piece that made the puzzle incomplete. And then it hit me. Although most courtship manuals never acknowledge that a woman may want to remain single, Faludi never acknowledges that she may want to marry. She fails to recognize that the pressure of the backlash is so effective not because the media controls us or because women are easily duped but rather because the conventions of marriage and motherhood tap into the real human need to love and be loved.

Exposing social pressure is important, especially if it helps women distinguish their own desires from societal expectations. But implying that a woman who longs for a male partner is simply the victim of a sexist plot does not help us discover our true selves; it simply adds to our insecurity.

While the dominant cultural wave sweeps women toward marriage, there is also an opposing undercurrent—the fear of being trapped in the traditional roles our mothers and older sisters discarded. Having recently discovered the joys of independence, women may be afraid to give them up. This anxiety can block discernment as much as anxiety about singleness.

Although the older women I interviewed all grew up expecting to marry, women in their twenties and thirties often received mixed messages. We were supposed to marry and have children, but we weren't supposed to *need* a man. We were supposed to look for a husband, but we weren't supposed to let anyone catch us looking. As a result, many of us feel double-edged anxiety. We fear what we will miss if we don't marry *and* what we'll give up if we do. We fear being alone *and* feeling trapped.

Fiona, for example, is proud of her independence. Twenty-eight years old with rich long hair and a Cambridge education, Fiona recoils from the thought of being dependent on anything. At the same time, she has always assumed that one day she would marry and have children, and sometimes she imagines how nice it would be to have a partner. Then she tells herself, "I shouldn't think like this. I should be independent!" Fiona explains, "It makes me uncomfortable to think I might be prey to society's acculturation, that because I'm a 'girl' I feel I ought to get married at some point." Because she is aware of the social pressure, she is mistrustful of her own longings and wary about meeting men. "There's this awful feeling of not wanting to be seen as a desperado," she explains. Although Fiona is outgoing and attractive, she sometimes acts cool and aloof when meeting men so she will not appear too eager for a relationship. She observes that this attitude can close her off to potential intimacy and that she is now trying to learn how to be open without being desperate.

In *Soul Mates: Honoring the Mysteries of Love and Relationship*, author Thomas Moore observes that the opposing desires for attachment and autonomy both come from the soul, and both must be honored. Moore asserts:

> As strong as the yearning for attachment is, there is obviously something else in us that yearns for solitude, freedom, and detachment. Our examination of relationship must include both sides of this spectrum and embrace the tension that may exist as we try to give attention to each.

Embracing this tension can be an important step for an individual who feels double-edged anxiety. It can also shed new light on social stereotypes about gender and commitment.

It's often assumed that women fear singleness and men fear marriage. This generalization disregards the many men who yearn for marriage and the many women who don't. Workshops I have led have often been evenly divided between men and women with the men just as eager to make a commitment and just as frustrated that they hadn't found the right person yet. Thirty-seven-year-old Larry has never been married but would like to be. A tall, thoughtful man who writes poetry and is part of a men's group, Larry consciously tries to be aware of his own conflicting emotions. "In my experience, most heterosexual men are pretty eager to be in relationships with women, and even to be married," he observes. "But I think there's a lot of naïveté about how much work the commitment involves. Men's fear comes in working through conflicts around intimacy. Sometimes that happens before getting married. Sometimes those conflicts don't surface until years later."

Larry notes that in his relationship with Susan, the gender roles were reversed. Larry and Susan had been living together for three years when it looked like she might be offered a job in London. Although Larry's job as executive director of a small nonprofit was very important to him, he was willing to follow her, a prospect she found terrifying. "When we were on the brink of a commitment, a part of her that I had never seen before came roaring out. It was a part I didn't like very much," he says. "The proximity of the commitment kicked up a lot of issues within her that she was in denial about and wasn't really interested in working on." She pulled away from the relationship, leaving Larry hurt and confused.

Larry reflects that it is natural to have conflicting feelings about something as major as marriage; the question is how to deal with them. "A sign of my maturity is recognizing and accepting my internal contradictions. Every person I know deeply has those contradictions." He says that therapy has helped him differentiate the various voices within himself so that he can accept each as a part of the integrity of the whole. "When there's an internal conflict, I sit down and survey the different perspectives I have. I use my journal a lot. I might use six different colors. I try to break it down. Then I get a better understanding of what's at stake."

Although clearly not all men fear commitment, I know so many cases where the woman was ready to marry before the man that I wonder if there is any truth to the stereotype. Perhaps there is something about maleness that includes a stronger yearning for independence. Carl Jung argued that there is a difference between "masculine" and "feminine" energy, and psychologists often label independence as a "masculine" trait. But Jung also argued that all people include both "masculine" and "feminine" attributes, and healthy people develop a balance between them. When we portray women as commitment seekers and men as commitment avoiders, we dishonor the opposing impulse in every soul. Couples sometimes fall into this trap, where one person acts as the force for togetherness and the other acts as the force for separateness. The more the one (stereotypically the woman) presses for commitment, the more the other (stereotypically the man) feels reluctant. His reluctance fuels her anxiety, and she presses harder. Thomas Moore's insight that all people need both attachment and independence can free couples from this dynamic, allowing each one to experience a fuller range of feelings toward their relationship.

Whether our urge for attachment outweighs our urge for independence is influenced by more than just gender. Did we see a healthy model of marriage growing up? Did we see a healthy model of singleness? What were the expectations within our family? Although television, movies, and magazines dominate popular culture, our family culture is influenced by race, religion, class, and ethnicity. Some spiritual and cultural traditions encourage marriage more strongly than others. For example, as Rabbi Marcia explained, in Judaism marriage is an important *mitzvah*, a spiritual imperative like keeping the Sabbath and learning Torah. Thus, for a practicing Jew, the desire to marry has a spiritual context that is different for someone from a tradition that considers singleness an acceptable alternative. Consequently, a Jewish man may feel a greater push to marry than, say, an African American woman.

Although neither Cheryl nor her Jewish family are religious, Cheryl believes family pressure was one of the reasons she married her first husband at the age of twenty-two. "I lived with him," says Cheryl, "and it was particularly hard on my father. That was hard on me because my father and I had always been close. Prior to that he had always understood my unconventional moves, and this was one he didn't understand. So there was a lot of pressure to get married because of that." Now forty and married to William, Cheryl realizes that when she married the first time, she did not yet know who she was in her own right. "But also for me," she recalls, "like many women of my generation, maybe even for women today, it was the natural step. You're expected to get married, so you get married." After her divorce, Cheryl realized that she would rather be alone than be in the wrong marriage, even though she was certain she wanted children. "That took me a long time and a lot of pain to get to," she recalls. Partly because she worked through this process, her decision to marry the second time was made freely and more consciously.

SORTING THROUGH OUR FEARS

When I graduated from college and flew off to Botswana as a Peace Corps Volunteer, I felt I could live anywhere, do anything. Although I was interested in men and relationships, any guy who got too close was a potential threat to my independence. During my twenties, I dated men who were either uninterested in long-term commitment or living thousands of miles away from me. These relationships were not the pathetic delusions of a commitmentphobe (as the courtship manuals and a few of my friends would suggest). They were my soul's way of embracing the tension between my need for attachment and independence. As I shifted into my thirties, however, my desire for attachment grew stronger. I traveled less. I acquired more houseplants. I wondered what it would be like to share my life with someone. After my relationship with Kevin, I began to seriously think about marriage as a vocation and wondered if I would ever feel called to partnership.

When I began writing this book, I focused on the backlash and women's fear of singleness, believing we must face this fear in order to discern if our desire to marry comes from calling or convention. A few months into my research, my perspective was broadened by an exercise in *If I'm So Wonderful, Why Am I Still Single?*—one of the only courtship manuals that encourages readers to look inward for answers. Author Susan Page, who has a master of divinity rather than the usual doctorate in psychology, suggests that we sit in silence, relax, close our eyes, and visualize that we are about to be married. As we imagine the scene, we are told to pay attention to our body and what it tells us about our emotions. Are we tense or relaxed? Happy or sad? After exploring these feelings, we are told to repeat the process, imagining we have made a firm decision never to marry.

I relaxed on the couch and closed my eyes to do the exercise. Then, panic! As I tried to visualize my impending wedding, I could feel my shoulders tense and my heartbeat quicken. My jaw was clenched and my breathing shallow. Even without a specific groom in mind, the prospect of marriage terrified me. "What if this is a mistake? What if we get bored with each other? What if he becomes paralyzed in a car accident and I have to empty his bedpan for the rest of my life?" At the heart of my fears was the question, "What if I feel trapped?" Like Fiona, I saw myself as strong and independent. The thought of losing my freedom was terrifying. When I envisioned being single for the rest of my life, my body relaxed notably. My shoulders loosened, my heartbeat slowed, and my breath deepened. Then I felt my eyes moisten, not crying but sorrowful. Being alone is something I know I can do, so it did not scare me. But I felt a deep sense of loss, like something was missing.

This exercise helped me appreciate the complexity of my emotions about marriage. While I was busy taking notes for this book—collecting a stack of index cards about women's fear of singleness—I was overlooking the evidence within me that fear of commitment is just as real. I decided to explore my feelings consciously so they would not rule my life subconsciously. If I married, I wanted it to be a calling to partnership, not running away from loneliness or attempting to conform socially. If I remained single, I wanted it to be because I had discerned a vocation to singleness, not because I was afraid of intimacy or commitment. I wanted to acknowledge all the pressures in my life and understand them so that my choices grew out of love, not fear.

In *The Art of Loving*, psychoanalyst Erich Fromm observed that *"while one is consciously afraid of not being loved, the real, though usually unconscious fear is that of loving."* This rings true to my experience. When I first completed the visualization exercise, I thought I feared being trapped, losing my independence; and I did. But on a deeper level, what I feared was real loving. I enjoyed the freedom to do what I pleased without considering anyone except myself, and I wasn't sure I wanted to give it up. Especially coming of age in the wake of the women's movement, I knew the freedom to be selfish was a luxury for women, a right only recently claimed, whereas the challenge of loving sounded suspiciously like the old feminine ideal. With few equal, loving partnerships as role models, I feared that being a loving wife meant becoming June Cleaver.

Having discarded June Cleaver as the paragon of femininity, many women today fear that they are unable to honor their true selves and love a male partner at the same time. In a Faith and Feminism class I took at Pendle Hill, this was an urgent discussion topic for several women who were in relationships with men. We wondered how much solitude we needed and if the men in our lives would accept this need. We wondered if we would deny our own callings when they brought conflict with our partners. We wondered if loving a man would keep us from fully loving God. We feared orbiting our lives around a man and losing our true selves in the process.

Women are conditioned to mold themselves into what others want and often do so in ways that men (or the women themselves) never notice. But acute awareness of this conditioning may also make us afraid to give or compromise, essential ingredients of a loving relationship. Patricia (who runs couples enrichment workshops with her supportive husband, Brad) complains that some books on women's spirituality, though inspirational in other respects, imply that spiritual growth for women is next to impossible within heterosexual partnership. She acknowledges that there are many women who have been stifled by confining marriages, but she states earnestly, "I acknowledge that reality is there, but I maintain that my experience is not unique. There are women out there who are great in part because of the support of their spouses." She says one day she would like to write her own book on women who have found growth and enrichment within heterosexual marriage.

Patricia's point brings us back to the concept of vocation and the importance of finding the way we are meant to grow as a lover. A woman who marries a man to fulfill social expectations despite a calling to some other lifestyle may experience her marriage as limiting. But another woman may find that marriage nurtures her growth as a person. It may even be the challenge of honoring her own needs *and* those of a male partner that teaches her to love God, self, and others more fully. Stifling a desire for partnership for fear of giving up our independence does not make us more liberated.

A few women I interviewed shared how hard it was for them to admit that deep down they really wanted to marry. Helen recalls, "Part of my struggle in life has been admitting that I'm looking for someone." During her twenties, Helen dated men of different religious backgrounds, an experience that helped her clarify her own beliefs and values. By her mid-thirties, however, Helen was eager to settle down with a permanent partner. She notes that it was one of the courtship manuals that helped her to acknowledge her longing. "After about five years where I didn't do a lot of dating, I read *How to Marry the Man of Your Choice*," recalls Helen. "I loved the beginning of it, in terms of how you get yourself out there and meet people. It was really valuable to me as a lesson in how to be open to people. I hated the rest of the book that got into how you manipulate this man down the aisle and how you turn yourself into the person he wants. But I loved the first part of the book, and so I very consciously used it and started meeting men left and right and went out on lots of dates. It was quite amazing." Now married, Helen notes that this was an important step for her. "There was something really freeing about admitting that I was looking for a partner and someone to share my life with." For women who secretly long for a male partner, affirming this desire may be a necessary part of their discernment process.

One common stumbling block to admitting our desire is insecurity about our physical attractiveness. Although both men and women may suffer from this worry, it is particularly intense for many women. The endless advertisements for makeup and diets reinforce the belief that how we look is more important than who we are or what we do with our lives. Particularly when it comes to romantic love, many of us have internalized the message that we have to look like supermodels in order to be worthy.

In high school, I was never one of the pretty girls; I was always one of the smart girls. I was yearbook editor, not prom queen. Actually, I wasn't even asked to the prom, a fact I made light of at the time but which fueled in me the fear that no boy would ever be interested in me, unless it was to help him with his math homework. As I grew into adulthood and experienced more male attention than I had in adolescence, I began to believe I was attractive, but even then with twinges of embarrassment that my skin wasn't smoother or my belly flatter. Today I know that real beauty comes from inside a person, and the times I feel most radiant are the times my inner light is shining most brightly. But old insecurities die hard, and still there are odd moments, usually when I feel uncentered or afraid, when the awkward high school girl who never got asked to the prom comes back to haunt me.

When I wrote about these feelings in an article a few years ago, several men commented to me how shocked they were that I felt this way. "Don't you know you're pretty?" they asked, as if their reassurance could undo years of cultural conditioning. I found it difficult to explain to them what women seemed to understand easily, that a generally self-confident woman with lots of talents and friends can still look at the cover of *Cosmo* and fear that she'll never be loved.

Although limited images of beauty may intensify our anxiety about finding a mate, the consumer model of love is the real basis of our fear. As long as we try to sell ourselves on the love market, we will feel like commodities to be advertised. As long as we think of love as scarce, we will fear being love-poor. Whether we feel insecure about our looks, our intelligence, our income, or some other quality we fear is lacking, we may need to acknowledge our insecurity before we can move through it to deeper self-acceptance. Only then can we focus on learning to love rather than trying to acquire love.

There are many personal experiences that may arouse our anxiety about relationships. If we have experienced rape or domestic violence, we may be afraid to let anyone too close. Or, conversely, we may need a greater degree of commitment in order to feel secure. If we are gay, seeking partnership means flying in the face of social expectations; we may risk losing family, friends, or employment. If we are divorced, we may fear repeating past pains and mistakes. Recognizing the factors that pull us toward or away from partnership is an important part of the process of discerning how we are meant to love.

Masking our anxieties hides our true selves. Perhaps we cultivate an image of independence to buffer ourselves from rejection. Or perhaps we feel content being single, but we feign interest in romance since that's what's expected. Perhaps we're attracted to members of our own gender, but we stifle these feelings rather than face homophobia. In any case, projecting a false self may shield our vulnerabilities, but it will also keep us from fully loving ourselves and others. Instead of denying our fears and desires, listening to them can help us understand our own motivations more deeply. The process of facing our fears can help us to grow as a lover.

We may have to face a variety of anxieties, as Amy's story

shows. The oldest of five children, Amy was hit hard by her parents' divorce. She acknowledges that watching her childhood family tear apart contributed to her fear of commitment. Still, the feeling that she should marry young and have children like her mother was deeply ingrained. Amy recalls, "I remember graduating from high school and thinking, 'If I'm not married by the age of twenty-five and having my first child, I'm a big loser.' So I gave myself a time limit." By the time she turned thirty, her younger brother and many of her peers were already married. Amy pressured her boyfriend, Ben, to propose, throwing hints about how much she would love a ring for Christmas. She got her ring but soon regretted it. "Like that old saying," she explains, "you have to be careful of what you wish for because you'll get it."

Canceling her engagement to Ben last year helped Amy overcome her panic and learn to trust her "gut." "I just knew that something was wrong," she says. Amy's instincts told her it was a mistake, so she followed them, despite the surprise of her friends. "The hardest thing was telling people," recalls Amy. "I had already bought the dress. We had to cancel the reservations for the church and the reception area. I just felt stupid." Through this process, Amy realized how she had pressured Ben and how the biological clock had pressured her. She observes that she now has a new attitude: "Motherhood is not something that has to fulfill me. It would be nice, but I don't have to have it now, which is good." Realizing that she doesn't want to marry the wrong guy in order to have children has removed her sense of time pressure about getting married.

In a sense, breaking off her engagement was the way Amy faced all her fears: affirming herself as a single person and risking the hurt of ending a long-term relationship. The result is that she has a deeper trust of her own intuition. She concludes, "Trust your gut. Trust your heart. When your internal self says, 'This is going down the wrong path,' you better listen."

THE BIOLOGICAL CLOCK

For many women, like Amy, the pressure of the biological clock compounds anxiety about finding a marriage partner. There are parental hints about grandchildren, articles on the dangers of postponing parenthood, and TV talk shows on anguished childless women. For those who hope to enjoy both marriage and motherhood, the increasing number of candles on the birthday cake may cause alarm. Every man becomes a potential father. Every failed relationship sounds another tick of the biological clock. The concern about age is not unfounded. Although men who postpone parenthood also risk infertility, men have a later and less predictable deadline than women, whose fertility generally decreases in their late thirties or early forties as the risk of birth defects increases. By forty-five, most women are unable to get pregnant.

Nancy always wanted to have children and a career, just like her physician mother. Now a thirty-two-year-old teacher who is halfway through her first pregnancy, Nancy recalls being startled when her older brother and sister-in-law couldn't conceive. "It never occurred to me that I ever had to worry about anything other than *not* getting pregnant when I didn't want to," she states. When Nancy had an irregular pap smear result at age twenty-three, she became terrified that she might have cancer and need a hysterectomy. She remembered sobbing in bed, "thinking of those times in college when I had desperately prayed for my period to start, and here I wasted all those chances to have a child. I totally freaked for about six hours. They did the biopsy, and it was fine," Nancy recalls. "That was my first moment of sampling that piece of fear. Then I started hearing about tons of women now who can't get pregnant, and I remember really being scared." Nancy points out that we hear more about infertility today partly because there are more fertility treatments available. Even so, she states, "All my life I had expected and planned on this, and I have no control over it. I actually have more control over whether I'm a teacher or a doctor than I do over whether or not I have a kid. That was very sobering."

Like the desire to marry, the desire to have children can be fueled by social expectations. Thirty-seven-year-old Betsy loves living alone in her quiet, book-filled apartment, and she has accepted the possibility that she may never marry or have children. Still she is aware how social pressure has affected her. "I always thought—raised in the fifties and sixties—that I, like every other healthy woman, would have children by now," she states. "But it has never felt strongly compelling in my life. I have never looked around and thought, 'Jeez, if only I had a child, it would really round things out nicely.'" A dedicated teacher, Betsy feels that in a world that is already overpopulated, it is wrong for people to have children merely to be conventional. Yet she acknowledges the pressure is strong: "I will probably be struggling for the rest of my life—just because I was raised in this culture—not to think of myself as less because I didn't give birth and raise a child."

Betsy notes that having nine nieces and nephews makes being single easier. "I'm not in the same situation as an only child whose parents are desperately waiting for grandchildren," she says. But she adds that her parents would be more comfortable if she were married because they know our society is more supportive of married women. "Now if you have a child, that knocks you up a whole other notch," she states. "I think a great deal of women's frenetic childbearing is because they get so little value in our society outside of being a wife and a child breeder." Betsy is angered by this limited view of womanhood: "If they want to put us in the caretaking role, let's fill the Department of the Interior with women. I'll take care of some things for you. I'd love to."

Although pressure to bear children certainly adds to women's anxiety, social pressure alone does not explain the allure of motherhood. Whether the urge is biological, spiritual, or both, it can be deep and compelling. For some women, motherhood is a vocation. For practicing Jews, having children is a *mitzvah*, a spiritual imperative. Women who do not use religious language may still yearn to experience the miracle of childbirth and think of it in spiritual terms. Like the desire to marry, the desire to bear children cannot be written off as a mere by-product of the backlash.

The desire for children may complicate our discernment about marriage. Who we consider as a partner, even the decision to marry itself, may be influenced by the prospect of parenthood. For some, children are the primary reason for the commitment of marriage. For others, the desire for children affects the timing of this choice, sometimes exerting painful pressure on both partners. I know one couple who were so tormented by the question of whether or not they should marry before the woman's upcoming fortieth birthday that their whole relationship seemed to consist of judging each other and evaluating their future prospects. The joy of nurturing each other's life and growth was lost in their anxiety about her aging ovaries, making it impossible for them to hear the deeper wisdom of their hearts.

The first step toward working through this anxiety is to acknowledge it to ourselves. If we want to bear children, we can begin by accepting this feeling, embracing it, listening to it, and trying to discern if it comes from our true self or the false self of conformity. If we assume that marriage and motherhood go together, we might want to examine this assumption to see if it stems from love of children or desire for social acceptability. If we think of marriage as a means to an end, we might ask ourselves what type of marriage this attitude will produce and how an unhappy or short-lived union might affect any resulting children. Becoming conscious of our own motivations helps us to seek the most loving path.

For Helen, admitting to herself that she was looking for a life partner was an important step. She had always longed to experience the miracle of giving birth, and she knew she wanted two parents for her children. Conscious that her fertile years would not last forever, she actively dated during her thirties, hoping to meet a mate soon. She reflects, "Much as I wanted a child, I was always really clear that I didn't want to do it in a way which was less than best for that child." For example, she was clear she wouldn't marry the wrong person just to have children or allow herself to "accidentally" get pregnant, even though she very much wanted a baby.

At thirty-nine, Helen met Raymond, the first man with whom she felt she could share her life. Since Raymond was forty-seven and also eager for children, concern about infertility pushed them to act quickly. "It threw us into a different stage of relationship," Helen comments. They began trying to get pregnant only a few months into their relationship and began fertility treatments before setting a wedding date. By the time they married, they were investigating options for adoption. Helen comments, "The point for me is that we chose to get married *knowing* we couldn't conceive." They realized they wanted to spend their lives together whether or not they could create a child together. "We were both clear that raising a child in a loving home was the greatest contribution we could make to the world," says Helen. "We both had to work through the desire to see our own genes imprinted on that child's face, but once we did, adoption became a marvelous alternative—one that in no way seems second best."

Helen and Raymond are now the joyful parents of an adopted baby boy. Although giving up her dream of biologically bearing a child included painful struggle, Helen feels confident that she made the right decisions along the way. She focused on what she felt was the greatest good, for herself and for a potential child, even though that meant letting go of an important aspect of what she wanted.

Facing the possibility of never bearing children can raise many emotions in women. For some, it brings tremendous sadness, grieving the loss of a lifelong dream. Others become aware of God's role in creating life and the limits of human ability to control that miracle. For others, letting go of the possibility of motherhood frees romantic relationships to develop under less pressure, without a perceived deadline for decision making. Infertility can also challenge people's perception of marriage as an arrangement primarily for the bearing and raising of children, encouraging them to seek the spiritual dimensions of partnership. It can also dramatically demonstrate that one's body is aging, fragile, mortal. In a society where female beauty is equated with youth and thinness, moving past fertility into menopause can shake a woman's sense of her sexual self.

Sue is forty-six and recently divorced. After twenty years of marriage, where her goals consistently took a backseat to her husband's medical career, he left her for a woman a few years older than their daughter. Sue reflects on how our culture's definition of female beauty affects her feelings about finding a new romantic relationship. "It's a real hurdle," she states. "In my situation, where my husband left me for a much younger woman, there can't help but be thoughts of, 'I'm too old. I'm not attractive.' I'm past my childbearing usefulness, so you start asking, 'Well, what good am I then?'" Sue describes the experience of "being cast off like an old shirt that's gotten frayed around the edges, and maybe the collar's a little too tight, so you just take it off and throw it away." She adds, "When you've been tossed off like a dirty shirt, sometimes it's hard not to feel like one."

Sue is struggling to accept her situation honestly, acknowledging that it is possible she may never marry again while at the same time admitting that she would like to. Speaking of her first husband and the years when they had a close, caring relationship, Sue says, "The way I met him was totally a gift, and a crazy set of circumstances which in my wildest imagination I couldn't have planned. So I have to have faith that if that is going to happen again, if there is supposed to be another marriage or another close relationship in my life, it will happen." She warns, however, that saying one should have faith is one thing, "but the reality of living that is a whole different ball game."

BEING ALONE

Part of what makes waiting with faith difficult is the reality of loneliness. When we are alone and lonely, we may think a partner will fill our emptiness. Rather than exploring the root of our inner need, we may focus on strategies to meet someone new or ways to improve our appearance. Like social pressure and the biological clock, loneliness may propel us toward partnership whether or not that is really the way we are called to love.

Our society frequently confuses loneliness with being alone, although they are very different experiences. I never feel lonely watching the sunset or walking in the woods. Alone in nature, my solitude is a gift that enables me to appreciate the grandeur of the earth. I can discard clever conversation and let my senses become more attuned: to the coldness of my nose or the color of the trees, to the blood pumping in my toes and thumbs, to the sound of the birds and the gurgling of the creek. In such moments, I know I am fully alive and part of a life much larger than I can comprehend. I return to human company vibrant and refreshed.

In contrast, my loneliest moments tend to be with other people: the dinner party where everyone is talking about redecorating; the crowded subway where no one makes eye contact; and, worst of all, the mall at Christmastime. I feel myself becoming shriveled and numb, trying to block out the frantic consumerism. I look at the haggard faces of holiday shoppers, weighed down with too many packages and bills, and the oversized ads in every shop window. The crowds and noise only add to my feeling of separation, and I rush through my errands, anxious to get home.

Feelings of desperate isolation are as old as humankind, and they do not seem to lessen as people live in closer physical proximity. If anything, our culture heightens our feelings of loneliness. Many feel surrounded by crowds, rather than community, and too few of us know our neighbors. This alienation contributes to many social problems: alcoholism, drug use, suicide, and our tendency to blare the television to drown out our pain. But drugs and alcohol provide only short-term relief, making us feel even more isolated when the high wears off; meanwhile, the television barrages us with advertisements showing blissful families in beautiful houses and neighbors bringing each other coffee. The contrast with our own lives can leave us feeling emptier than before. Such advertising images surround us. As we sit in traffic on the way to work, billboards filled with frozen smiling faces gnaw at our hearts, making us suspect that everyone else has found a happiness we have not.

In addition to the dull ache of isolation, there is also the specific feeling of being lonely for an intimate romantic relationship. My most powerful experience of this came several years ago when a friend invited me to an Irish dance, or *ceili*, where her boyfriend was playing the fiddle. When I arrived, she was busy with the musicians and couldn't sit with me, so to compensate she deposited me with a middle-aged couple she knew at one of the side tables. The announcer called people to line up for the first dance, and the woman kindly offered to lend me her husband. We joined a line of couples, and a dance began which was vaguely similar to the Virginia Reel I had learned in Girl Scouts. The ballroom was soon full of swinging and laughing, and my partner skillfully kept me from knocking over any neighbors. I was just getting the hang of it when the band sounded the final chord, and he thanked me for the dance. I smiled broadly, my face flushed and damp, and we walked back to the table.

As the couple headed to the floor for the next reel, I scanned the rest of the room to see who else was sitting this one out. A quick glance around the tables made it clear that everyone had come in couples, and there was not a man in sight who looked likely to dance with me. I remained on the sidelines, tapping my feet to the music through a reel, a jig, and then a waltz. This was not like the dances I was used to where a crowd of people weave and bob in the dark, barely looking at each other. There you don't need a partner. The crowd absorbs a loner or a group of friends dancing together. But here, where every set required an equal number of men and women, my single status barred me from the dance floor. I became annoyed that my friend had not warned me. If I had known, I would have invited a partner. And then it hit me: Who could I have asked?

My throat tightened as tears began to fill my eyes. Only a month before I had said good-bye to a man I deeply loved as he headed back to his home in South Africa. I was unsure if I would ever see him again, and there was not another man in the world whom I would want to invite to a dance. I stood up and headed for the door, past the twirling couples, out to the cool night air. I hurried to my car and pulled into the heavy Friday night traffic. Tears were streaming down my face by the time I reached the first red light. Two blocks later, I was sobbing uncontrollably and had to pull the car over to the side of the road.

The memory of this evening is painful, and even with several years' hindsight, writing about it was difficult. As I sat in front of my computer, reliving the details, I unconsciously devoured half a package of cookies. I finally realized what I was doing and stopped myself after the sixth Pecan Sandie. Appropriate, in a sense, for this is what the struggle is all about: acknowledging the aching, empty places in ourselves and resisting the temptation to fill them up with junk food, alcohol, or shallow romantic affairs. Overcoming loneliness means facing the painful moments of isolation without running to the refrigerator. It means outgrowing the expectation of easy comforts and quick solutions.

Quick solutions are big business, however. Product advertisements imply that if we buy the right brand of toothpaste (or car, or coffee, or mouthwash) a perfectly gorgeous man (or woman) will walk, smiling, into our lives. This promise is even less subtle when it comes to beauty products. We face ceaseless images of smiling, skinny, flawless models selling diet programs, liposuction, and $60 facial cream. Then there are the businesses that explicitly promise to end loneliness, from singles networks to newspaper classifieds. At least one video dating service claims 160,000 members nationwide. Membership requires a commitment of between $1,000 and $2,000.

At the center of the problem is the myth that if we find someone we won't be lonely anymore. No doubt this promise makes the disillusionment all the more poignant when the myth fails to be true. Wearing a gold ring does not end loneliness. In fact, the despair of loneliness can be even greater when we feel isolated within marriage.

Loneliness is not confined to single people or those with bad marriages, as Pat and her husband, Tom, attest. Pat and Tom have a close marriage that nurtures their work in a poor urban neighborhood, and they laugh at many points during our interview, describing how God brought them together when they least expected it. But when we reach the topic of loneliness Pat's tone becomes serious. "Just by our very nature of being on this earth, we are lonely," she states. "We will always be lonely. In the midst of the greatest love in the world, we will be lonely. I have experienced excruciating lonely, separate times, and Tom is sitting right there. But inside me, I've been so estranged, and I feel myself pulling away. It's my own stuff that I have to deal with, and no human being alive can fill that space. Nobody. And it isn't right to encourage the expectation that they can."

Tom, a Presbyterian minister near retirement, nods and adds that loneliness is a gift to be worked with, not avoided. Pat concurs: "The lonely space is an opportunity for God to commune with me." When we avoid loneliness by keeping our lives full of distractions, she asserts, we leave no room for God. "Maybe that's, to a large extent, why there is that void in us, that sense of nothingness, because we don't allow that lonely time to ferment."

Allowing the loneliness to ferment means discovering the parts of us that feel incomplete and accepting them with tenderness. It is often in times of weakness that we are able to recognize God and find comfort in the fact that the world does not revolve around our meager efforts. For me, time spent alone in nature—in the woods, atop a mountain, by the sea—always puts my problems in perspective. I come away with a clearer sense of my own value and a deepened sense of connection to the world around me. Similarly, Kathryn, whose vocation to singleness includes times of penetrating loneliness, says that it is in facing her aloneness that she finds growth: "If I continue to listen to God, God changes that loneliness into solitude. And that's where God is, in that solitude."

The connection between solitude and spiritual growth is well established throughout human history. Moses went up the mountain and spent time alone in prayer. So did Jesus. Mohammed spent long periods alone in the desert. Quieting the mind was one of the Buddha's central teachings. No matter how it is defined theologically—prayer, listening to God, centering, emptying—most religions have some tradition of solitude and quiet reflection. In today's hectic world, the need for periods of quiet and solitude seems greater than ever. Time to notice the sacred and pay attention to it. Time to listen to our inner voice.

Time to allow questions and inspirations to emerge at their own pace, without competition from the car pool schedule or the ringing telephone.

Many think that solitude isolates us from other people, yet actually it does the opposite. Solitude helps us know ourselves, which in turn makes our intimate relationships more healthy. We become less likely to burden our partner with the impossible expectation that she will meet our every need, heal every wound, and fill every emptiness. By respecting our separateness, we allow the individual growth that nurtures our togetherness. As the German poet Rainer Maria Rilke wrote, "A good marriage is that in which each appoints the other guardian of his solitude." Especially for women, who have so often been told that we need a man to legitimize us, it is helpful to face our ultimate solitude and embrace it before we attempt to embrace another.

There is little in our society, however, that encourages us to let our loneliness ferment into solitude. Television seems designed to numb people to their loneliness, drowning out the uncomfortable thoughts that might arise if we were left in silence. It is a cheap anesthetic, always there, if not to listen to our troubles, at least to distract us with someone else's. Perhaps this explains the popularity of talk shows on "Deadbeat Boyfriends" and "Men Who Are Dogs." Watching these shows, our relationship (or lack of one) may not seem so bad. Even the evening news played during the car ride home from work helps us forget the dullness of our jobs and our yearning for something more in life.

When we do face our uncomfortable thoughts, we begin to realize how alone we ultimately are and how little we are understood. Even if we have a loving spouse, a supportive family, caring friends, we still enter and leave this world basically alone. A glimpse of this truth can send us scrambling for distractions—a trip to the mall, the bar, the gym, the movies. Noble pursuits are particularly deceptive diversions. When our days are filled with feeding the homeless, whipping up cookies for the church bake sale, and teaching Girl Scouts how to macramé, we feel assured that we are doing good and don't have time to wonder if we could be doing better. Excessive busyness can protect us from difficult questions about the purpose of our lives, but avoiding these questions also constricts our growth and wholeness.

Even if we savor times of quiet and solitude, we may still assume that we need another person to complete us. Irene married in 1959 and spent seventeen years trying to become the wife her husband wanted. Now with twenty years' hindsight, she describes her divorce as "a kind of resurrection," leading to a period of dramatic spiritual growth. Yet she recalls, "When I divorced, I was still enough of a child of my generation that I just assumed I would get married again." In the ten years after her divorce, Irene had four significant relationships with men. "I would somehow put myself into orbit around these people, and it was always a terrible, terrible mistake," she states. One day, ten years ago, when the courtship dance had begun again, Irene stopped and questioned what she was doing. "Looking at the four men and at the husband, I said to myself, 'You have really rotten judgment! Don't you think it's about time for something different?'" Irene decided that she was "out of the handmaiden business." Although she didn't rule out the possibility of a future romantic relationship, she was clear that she was not going to orbit herself around a man again. This decision helped her center her life around God and grow in her love of solitude.

For Irene, an important turning point came when she

stopped focusing on men and focused instead on her inner growth. Several women interviewed related similar moments of deciding not to seek a romantic relationship for a while in order to focus on inner searching. For some, like Irene, singleness became a way of life. For others, a period of intentional singleness became important preparation for later relationships.

Elizabeth's life illustrates several of the issues explored in this chapter. Elizabeth, who came of age in the 1960s, recalls, "In my senior year of high school, I told people I did not want to get married ever, because I wanted a career. I assumed I had to accept my mother's view of being married, which was making a career as a homemaker." Elizabeth's aversion to marriage was strengthened by observing her older sister. "She spent six years—from the time she was fifteen till she was twenty-one—getting brides magazines and planning her wedding. Then she and my mother drove each other crazy for a year actually planning this wedding. I thought for sure somebody was going to be killed before it happened. So I didn't want to go near a church, certainly not in a white dress."

Elizabeth met Dave at age seventeen, and their relationship became more serious over the next three years. "Dave and I had both made statements about never wanting to get married and being afraid particularly of having our independence compromised. I think that was part of the attraction," she states. "We were both extremely stubborn, extremely independent, determined to live life on our own terms. We had a very good marriage because we went into it with those expectations," says Elizabeth, recalling how their conversations about marriage shifted from "never" to "not yet." "At one point he said to me, 'I know I'm not ready to be married now, but if I ever am ready, I want to ask you.' So one day he called and said, 'I'm ready to be married, and I want you to consider being married. If you're not ready, I'll wait till you are ready.' " Elizabeth, who had also been thinking about the issue, laughs, remembering how quickly she answered, "I'm ready!" They eloped soon afterward, skipping the brides magazines and the white dress.

Elizabeth and Dave supported each other through the growth of both their careers and the raising of children. They were married for over twenty years when he died leaving her a widow at the age of forty-three. "It hit me a few months after he died that I had never lived alone in my life," says Elizabeth, remembering the difficult transition. She was particularly surprised by the pressure she felt to quickly remarry. "About a month after my husband died, my neighbor was planning a singles' party, and she thought she was doing me a great favor to invite me, even though I told her I wasn't interested. She was very persistent and came to the conclusion, I think, that I didn't want to come because I didn't have the right thing to wear or something," laughs Elizabeth.

It was less than a year before Elizabeth felt happy living alone and felt at peace with the possibility that she might never have another intimate or sexual relationship. Ironically, it was after she came to this peace that an eight-year-old friendship gradually grew romantic. "At some point," says Elizabeth, "I realized I wanted the friendship to develop into a partnership, and yet I liked the way things were so much that I didn't want to put that pressure on myself or on him. So I found myself praying, and my prayer was, 'Guide me. Guide us. Help us to know what will be right for us and for our relationship.' I think that's really been helpful." Elizabeth states that she only wants to marry again if she and her partner both discern that it is the right thing to do. But thinking of the usual social assumptions she concludes, "That is a different way of looking at it, isn't it?"

Chapter Four

Letting Go

We can resist social pressure and recognize our own desires, but these steps do not necessarily reveal our vocation. Discernment requires moving beneath what we want right now to listen to the inward teacher, the true self's link with God. If in the deep core of our soul we feel called to partnership, then that may indeed be how God is calling us. But until we feel called to marry a specific person who also feels called to marry us, our discernment is tentative and incomplete.

If partnership is our vocation, God will help us find the right partner at the right time. It may not be the person or the time we expect, however. We may need to wait until the time is right. Or we may need to make some effort to reach out to others. Knowing when to wait and when to act is often a challenging aspect of discernment, but in the realm of romance it can be particularly confusing. By its nature, falling in love is not something we can schedule or control. It is a process that calls us to let go, particularly to let go of fear.

BE NOT AFRAID

A friend recently said, " 'Be not afraid.' That's the whole point of the Bible," and her comment stuck to me like a tenacious burr. I found myself thinking of those words as I listened to reports of violence on the evening news, realizing how many bombings and massacres are motivated by fear. I began noticing many situations where people's most destructive behavior comes from desperation and anxiety, fear of losing their property or their self-image. I could see it in myself, too. Thinking back to the most difficult periods of my life, I realized that it was usually fear that got in my way and made things worse.

Fear is most powerful when we are trying to prove we are not afraid. Unacknowledged fear stalks the shadows of the unconscious, exerting its influence subversively. That is why it is important to acknowledge the pressures in our lives, such as social stereotypes and the biological clock. By admitting our fears we peel away a layer of our false selves. By moving through our fears we grow in our capacity to love.

Part of the challenge of discernment is to understand which of our fears protect us and which hinder us. As a mother deliberately teaches a child to be afraid of fire or busy traffic, God also give us fear to protect us from danger. But we sometimes hold on to our protective armor long after it is useful. Realizing we are afraid of doing something does not clarify whether or not we should do it. Our anxiety may be a protective instinct, or it may point us in the direction we need to grow. Although we should not be ruled by our fears, we ignore them at our peril.

I became convinced that fear blocks human connection during three years of working as a door-to-door canvasser for a grassroots political organization. Each night we went to different neighborhoods, talked to people about issues like national health care and insurance reform, and asked them to write a check. How people responded was greatly affected by my attitude. On evenings when I focused only on the money, afraid of missing my $120 quota, people showed little interest. "Not tonight," "My wife has the checkbook," and "I gave at the office" became the ceaseless, numbing responses. Conversely, when I rang the doorbell with confidence, trusting the basic goodness and concern of the people I was approaching, the response was incredible. Strangers welcomed me into their homes, shared their stories, and gave generously.

If the evening got off to a bad start and I started to worry about my performance, every knock at the door became difficult. I could feel my jaw tighten and hear my voice get higher. People sensed my anxiety and refused to write a check to a nervous stranger. At such times, I needed to take time out. I sat down on the curb, placed my clipboard beside me, and looked up at the sky, letting my frustration seep into the grass. After a few minutes, I could feel the weight lift. The crease left my forehead; my muscles slackened. And only when my jaw was loose and my smile sincere would I stand up, brush myself off, and head for the next doorbell. Sometimes I would consciously decide that I didn't care how much money I made. My only goal was to have a positive interaction with every person. Suddenly there was a measurable improvement in my communication with people. Trust began to flow in both directions. On one frustrating evening, I raised a grand total of $5 in three hours, particularly humiliating since I had a first-day trainee observing me. At 8 P.M. I finally gave up all hope of saving my pride and decided to forget about the money. Then, to my surprise, I raised $115 in the next forty-five minutes. Canvassers across the country have had similar experiences.

The longer I canvassed, the more I could see the same principles at work in other areas of my life, especially in my relationships with men. When I was lonely and desperate for a date, no one was interested in me. When I tried too hard to act attractive or clever, guys never called back. On the other hand, when I was feeling confident and happy by myself, men were attracted to my energy and wanted to get to know me. When I wasn't trying to close a deal to meet my love quota, it was much easier to connect.

When I began doing interviews for this book, I sought out people I respected, those whose marriages I admired or who I thought had something profound to say on the subject of courtship. To my surprise and delight, I found my canvassing experience echoed in story after story. Although the details differed greatly, most of the women who identified themselves as "happily married" met their partners when they were relaxed about the prospect of marriage. Some had decided not to marry. Others knew they wanted to marry but had let go of the belief that they could force it to happen. For some, prayer and discernment were conscious parts of the process, for others not.

For example, Nancy always expected she could have marriage, children, and a career just like her physician mother. "When I was in high school, I actually planned out my life. I was going to marry a minister because, although I didn't believe in God, I wanted to marry someone who had a career I could respect," she laughs. "I was going to be a doctor by the time I was twenty-four, marry a minister by the time I was twenty-six, and at twenty-seven have my first kid. It was all very concrete. I can remember hitting twenty-seven; I was a teacher, and I'd never really met a minister. There was no marriage on my horizon, and there was no kid on my horizon. And I remember on my twenty-seventh birthday being horrified that my life had moved so far away from what I had wanted it to be."

Afraid of infertility after her brother and sister-in-law had been unable to conceive, Nancy began dating a man who had many of the qualities on her checklist. "We definitely were both on the family track," she states, "but I wasn't really in love with him. I think we both hit a point where we really grappled with whether you settled for what you had because it was okay, or whether you tried for something better. It terrified me that I would think that way," says Nancy. Eventually, they both realized that they were not ready to settle, so they ended the relationship.

At that point Nancy decided that if she reached thirty without meeting someone she really wanted to spend her life with, she would have a child on her own. "That took the pressure off," she explains. She decided not to date anyone for a while in order to take stock of her life and rethink where relationships fit. During this time she met her husband, Rick, when someone suggested they carpool to a conference. The two clicked during the two-hour ride, but Nancy was ambivalent about getting involved and gave Rick mixed messages for the first few weeks. Thinking about it now, she observes, "It amuses me that when I was least looking, it was easiest."

I ask her why it was easier then. "I think there's something to be said for taking that stress off yourself," Nancy answers, explaining that when she was really looking for a relationship, she was constantly evaluating her friendships with men to determine their romantic potential. "When I wasn't focused on it, and I was a little more relaxed, it happened more easily."

It is a paradox that life becomes easier once we stop trying so hard. When we are afraid of stuttering during a speech, that is exactly what we do. Fear of insomnia keeps us up at night. Anxiety about standardized tests makes it harder to answer the questions. The importance of attitude is especially recognized by athletes, who know that self-doubt can be more thwarting than any opponent.

If we look at love as something we must achieve, the pressure can make us incapable of loving. Even more than sports or public speaking, loving demands that we give up our self-absorption. Loving challenges us to see the world from another point of view. It forces us to care about another's wants and needs as well as our own. If we see a man as a prize to be won, rather than as a human being to be nurtured, we keep the focus on ourselves and our own efforts. What earrings should I wear? What amusing story should I tell? What time should I say good night? But the more we try to impress, the less we are likely to connect. If we strive to win a man, rather than enjoy him, we are likely to do neither. Whether he's conscious of it or not, the man will probably know the difference.

Nelson, for example, was always uncomfortable around single women until he met Marian. Now married almost fifty years, the two tease and correct each other as they recount the beginning of their courtship during World War II. At twenty-four, Marian had been a bridesmaid nine times and was self-conscious about her weight. As a leader of young Quakers in Philadelphia, it became clear to her during the summer of 1944 that she had something to offer the world, and it wouldn't matter whether she ever married or not. "Well, that fall, I had more dating than I had ever had in my life," she recalls.

Nelson, who was thirty-one at the time, had known Marian before, but his interest was sparked in December of 1944 when they met at a dance. "I danced with Marian, and she felt very good. And she looked very good. And the girl that I went to the dance with had already tried to change me. She told me I should part my hair differently," recalls Nelson with a grimace. But Marian seemed different. She was engrossed in her work. She wasn't anxious to get married or to change Nelson. "Here was a person that I felt very comfortable with," he recalls, "and I had been uncomfortable with others."

Nelson was comfortable with Marian because Marian was comfortable with herself. She knew she had something to offer the world. She didn't need a husband to make her happy. Ironically, this made her a more attractive partner. For Marian, the turning point came when she learned to trust herself. For my childhood friend, Mary, a similar shift occurred when she began to trust God.

"I remember the day my mother brought my little sister home from the hospital when I was four years old," says Mary. "I *knew* way back then that having kids and raising a family was what I wanted." During college, Mary's desire to make motherhood her career put a lot of pressure on her relationships with men. She recalls the stress of "always wondering, every time you dated someone, whether this was the guy you were going to marry or not." As a result, Mary often got more emotionally involved in a relationship than was appropriate, hoping it would lead to marriage. "A lot of times that's why we broke up," she explains, "because they were scared off."

At twenty-three, Mary reached a turning point. After ending a short relationship, she said to herself, "I'm not going to do this any longer." Serial dating was too painful. She still wanted to marry and begin a family, but she decided to trust that she didn't need to force it to happen. She lay in bed at night and asked God to help her recognize the right person. This eased her anxiety, and she stopped searching, spending more time with family and friends. It was through friends that she met her husband a few months later. Recalling their first date, swimming and then dinner, Mary says, "I wore nothing out of the ordinary, no makeup, and my hair was all wet. We went out to dinner, so I put on a bandanna. It didn't seem to matter what I looked like, which was really cool. We just hit it off from there. But it's funny how I really wasn't interested in dating anyone anymore, and there he was."

Sitting with her third daughter cradled in her lap, Mary explains that her faith that God would help her recognize the right person came largely from her mother. "She always said to me, 'Mary, just wait. There's a plan. You will meet the one you're suppose to meet when you're ready to.' She didn't necessarily bring God into it. She didn't say to me, 'When God's ready for this baby to be born, it will be born.' She always said, 'When the apple's ready, it will fall.' But I knew what she meant."

LETTING GO AND LETTING GOD

Many spiritual traditions recognize the wisdom of relaxing our anxious efforts. The old adage "Let go and let God" reminds us that we cannot force life to unfold as we wish. We are more likely to find peace if we become attuned to the greater cosmic rhythms, trusting the abundance of the universe. Inherent in this approach is the assumption that there is something greater than ourselves at work, a transcendent force of which we are only a part. When we stop grasping for control and open ourselves to what might come, we make it easier for the transcendent to break through and surprise us.

"Letting go and letting God" is not one more strategy for attracting men. The forces that bring two people together are too mysterious for such crude tactics. Who can explain why Nancy and Rick were given each other's phone numbers at that precise moment in their lives? Or why Nelson felt so comfortable with Marian? Who can know what would have happened if Mary had met the man she married two months earlier when she was still "looking"? Although letting go of their anxiety may have opened these women to the possibility of real intimacy, it would be overly simplistic to explain the growth of love in their lives as simple cause and effect.

Letting go of anxiety does not guarantee that we will get what we want. In my canvassing experience, taking a break and relaxing *usually* enabled me to meet my nightly quota, but not always. There were times when, no matter what I did, I just couldn't raise $120. Those nights were painful experiences of failure, but in retrospect, I see those failures as my teachers. They helped me begin to see my own perfectionism and my fear of admitting weakness. They showed me how dishonest I could be in hiding my vulnerabilities, not just at work but in my personal life as well. As a result, I now know myself better and am more capable of sharing my hurts in intimate and work relationships. Perhaps most important, I learned that failure and struggle can have positive effects. Today I believe that my periods of frustration as a canvasser were necessary fertilizer for my spiritual growth.

Learning that growth can come from struggle helps us trust the mystery of abundance. Painful experiences can crack open a mask, allowing a more whole person to emerge. As we let go of the false self, the person we thought we were, our illusion of independence disappears. Letting go on the deepest levels means allowing oneself to be transformed.

A quiet, prayerful presence, Rebecca quotes a verse from the Hebrew scripture to explain how she discovered her vocation to motherhood. "We are clay on the potter's wheel," she begins. "Every now and then God sees fit to take us, lump of clay, off and squeeze it all together again and start over on the potter's wheel." Coming of age in the early seventies, Rebecca was among the first generation of women who assumed she could "have it all." She married at twenty-four and had her first child, Anna, two weeks after completing her master's degree. But becoming a mother was deeply challenging in ways Rebecca had not anticipated. "I was being reformed," she says, "and I didn't like it. I resisted it. I remember reading *Mothering* magazine and feeling repulsed by what I would read there, like motherhood would demand *everything* if you really did it well, and there would be no time for anything else." Rebecca felt unable to bond with her infant daughter. She explains, "I was terrified of her. I sometimes would sit and look at her in the cradle and weep because I felt so overwhelmed. I knew *nothing* about the choice I had entered into out of just sheer enthusiasm and loving life and goodwill. Yet there was a tug about Anna, about the kind of work it really took to be present to her, when I could let go of all the other ambitions and aspirations."

A part-time teacher of religion, Rebecca explains, "Because the spiritual disciplines all say 'Let go and let God,' I dutifully tried to let go and let God, out of the obedient student part of me." Through this struggle, Rebecca recalls thinking, " 'There's something I'm not getting about the spiritual discipline of letting go and letting God and the privilege of loving.' I remember making a choice to say, 'All right, I will let myself learn.' It was like a little yes to an unknown. And that's what even opened up the possibility of a second child." Rebecca began to spend more time waiting and listening in the quiet. "It was marvelous," she recalls. "I actually did have an experience of a second child wanting to come, down to the week of knowing when to try. In saying yes to the second child, I was saying yes to the vocation of motherhood. I was very conscious of that," she states.

"It's a choice to yield," Rebecca explains, "like a piece of clay being reshaped. You have to give to that for it to happen. It's not an if-then prescription—let go and let God and then you get what you want. It's a very deep calling to a way of life. It means being willing for something in life to surprise you which can't happen if you're too busy shuffling all the cards. And yet we're not meant to just lie down and do nothing. Knowing where we are and what we want is part of our responsibility. But we're very little in that. We're tiny. It's like that quote, 'Lord, your sea is so large and my boat is so small.' I've got to be in my boat, and I've got to be paddling. But it's in this infinite ocean. I would just be ludicrous to think that I *knew* fully and completely what was best for me beyond a certain point."

Knowing ourselves is part of our responsibility. Just as unacknowledged fear can be most powerful, so unacknowledged desires can be most tenacious, exerting their power through the unconscious until we are forced to recognize them. Sorting through our insecurities and bringing our authentic desires to the surface is an essential step in discernment. Knowing who we really are helps us understand who we are meant to be and how we are meant to grow as a lover. Yet knowing that we are unable to see the whole ocean helps us stop trying to control the waves. We can trust that our real needs will be met, though maybe not in the way we expect. We can hold up to God the essence of our request (for example, love) and let go of our yearning to control the particulars (as in, I want this man to marry me by June).

My favorite image of letting go is an open, upward-facing hand. An open hand does not crush the object of its desire; nor does it push it away. It remains receptive without grasping. While I was trying to let go of Kevin, I shaped the image of an open hand out of clay. The experience was cathartic, forcing me to open my own hands as I held the delicate clay fingers, shaping their knuckles and nails. Others who saw the hand interpreted it as a symbol of giving or receiving rather than letting go, a reminder that an open hand invites more possibilities than one that is closed. I later learned that in Chinese calligraphy the symbol for letting go is also translated as "opening oneself to something new."

Letting go does not mean that we repress or deny our desires; we simply ungrasp them. We acknowledge that there may be something new trying to get into our lives that we won't be able to receive without the ungrasping. For example, Helen always wanted to give birth to a child, and her struggles with infertility included a long, painful process of letting go of what she most wanted. Once she did, however, she was blessed with an adopted baby boy whom she loves wholeheartedly.

Sometimes letting go means accepting something difficult or painful. A dramatic example is the story of Jesus in the garden of Gethsemane before his arrest and crucifixion. In anguish, Jesus prayed, "Father, if thou art willing, remove this cup from me; nevertheless not my will, but thine, be done." Jesus acknowledges his preference and at the same time opens to the possibility that he may not get it. After my decision to seek a spiritual approach to relationships, I began trying to imitate this form of prayer, acknowledging to God that I wanted an intimate partnership and at the same time saying, "If that is your will for me." There were times my words were only half sincere, but there were also moments where I really felt the desire to live however I was called, no matter what that meant.

Letting go is not easy. We cannot force it, fake it, or do it before we are ready. Sometimes, despite our best intentions, we feel clinging and grasping, and no amount of determination to let go can force us to feel at peace. We may even need to let go of our desire to let go, trusting that peace will come with time.

Although peace is ultimately a gift we must wait for, there are things we can do to ease the process. When I was having a bad night canvassing, the most helpful thing I could do was sit down and take a break. Acknowledging my frustration often eased the tension. I have found the same process helpful in my life. Taking a break—whether it is a long walk in the woods or a weekend silent retreat—is the best thing I can do when I feel anxious. Quiet time alone gets me in touch with my own emotions, and it also gets me in touch with something deeper. Natural beauty in particular, like mountains or an ocean, rekindles my sense of spiritual connection and reminds me that all great things take time. Nature reminds me to be patient.

A HAND IN DESTINY

Carolyn married twice, despite the internal voice warning her not to, because she wanted the security of marriage. Now finalizing her second divorce, Carolyn has dedicated her life to God and her Pentecostal church. When asked about the possibility of another marriage in the future, Carolyn says laughing, "I would have to hear it from the voice of God himself! I'm not going out looking for a husband, that's for sure!"

Through two difficult marriages and years of struggle, Carolyn learned to rely on God rather than men. "Whatever my needs, God is going to provide," she says seriously, pointing out that God sent Adam a helpmate without Adam asking. "If God sees that I need a helpmate, He's going to provide one for me. He may not be what I *want*. I may want a tall, handsome man. God may send me a little short, bald-headed man. But He's going to send me what is *best* for me. I don't have to look for it." Her voice begins to crescendo, like an evangelical preacher, as she emphasizes her point. "I don't have to look because if he's for me, God is going to make sure I get him. And I believe He's going to let me know if this helpmate is for me. I believe that with my whole heart."

Feeling called to partnership before one has found a partner raises profound questions about how God works in individual lives. Should we let God be the matchmaker, as Carolyn suggests? Or does God help those who help themselves? Will Mr. Right appear with a note of introduction from the Almighty? Or do we sometimes need to go out and look for him? Carolyn has two grown children and is expecting her fifth grandchild. Although only forty-two, she feels at peace with the possibility that she may never be with a man again. For a woman who still hopes to have children, waiting in peace may be more difficult. She may even feel she is called to look for a partner.

To relate to the Divine is to live in the tension between being passive and being active, to know when to wait and when to act. This applies to any discernment, but in the case of marriage the boundaries between our responsibility and God's are particularly confusing. If I feel called to attend law school, I know I have to send in an application. God is not going to fill in the form for me. But applying for a husband is not so clear-cut. Feeling a call to marriage can be extremely frustrating if we have not yet found a partner. The dating industry profits from this frustrated desire by selling all kinds of strategies for meeting new people.

"Your social life is not up to fate. It's up to you," argues *Guerrilla Dating Tactics*, a book that offers a strategic plan for ambushing someone at a party, including an aerial view diagram with dotted lines laying out a proposed patrol course. To meet someone wealthy, *How to Marry the Rich* suggests studying the obituaries and six months later applying for a job at the widower's office. "It is not, as some may think, immoral to take a hand in one's own destiny," defends *More Love Tactics*: "There is nothing wrong with using tactics in the pursuit of love." After all, the authors argue, "*All's fair in love and war.*"

The concept of taking a hand in one's own destiny challenges us to consider what it means to be a person of faith. For me, accepting that there is a Higher Power in the universe means accepting that I am not in control. My destiny is not entirely in my own hands. This does not mean that I am powerless, or that what I do does not matter. Rather, it means that what I want and what I do are not the only things that matter. It means moving from a narcissistic, or me-centered, view of life to one which leaves room for the mysterious workings of the Divine.

This attitude runs counter to secular, capitalistic culture, which promotes autonomy and individualism. The idea that we need to take control of our lives, pull ourselves up by our bootstraps, and forge ahead is deeply ingrained. This value is reflected in words like "self-sufficient," "self-reliant," and "self-made," which imply that a strong self is all we really need. In my view, it is literally impossible to be "self-made," not only because each of us relies on other human beings, but because ultimately we are all made by God. The role of the Divine is missing from "self-help" books, which focus only on what we can do to take control of our lives.

In contrast, churches or traditional religious figures often preach that one should give up one's own will entirely. My mother still repeats the message given to her in Catholic school by a strict nun with a thick Irish brogue: "You were put on this earth to suffer for the glory of Christ, and the sooner you get used to it the better off you'll be!" Although certainly this does not reflect the teachings of all religious leaders, it is an approach that has been taught all too often. Taken to the extreme, such attitudes can keep people silent through domestic violence, economic exploitation, and many other forms of repression. This is not the kind of yielding I advocate.

The ideal of suffering in silence that my mother grew up with has not changed as much as we might like to think, particularly for women. Women are still told that being quiet and passive makes them attractive to men. Some courtship manuals council their female readers to bite their tongues when a boyfriend criticizes them. Others advise always letting the man make the first move sexually, even after years of marriage. Even magazines aimed at young professional women suggest letting the man control the first date. *Passive patience is the feminine way,"* explains *Getting to "I Do."*

Paige, who is an atheist, a feminist, and a political activist, rejects the idea of submitting to a transcendent God or to a patriarchal culture. Yet despite her outspokenness on political issues, Paige notes that her sexist conditioning has made her more passive in sexual relationships. "I think, because I'm female, and I'm suppose to wait by the phone for it to ring, I tend to respond to people who have already decided that they are attracted to me. Somebody is interested in getting to know me, so suddenly I want to get to know them. I respond to what someone else wants." Paige reflects that this feeling may stem from her earliest experience of sex as a young adolescent trying to please an older boy. "I don't understand that yet, but I know that there's an element of passivity in waiting. It's not just waiting for something to happen, but not feeling like I have the right to say no. That can be a struggle for me. I don't take the space to decide if that is what I want."

Paige's struggle with her sexist conditioning points to the difference between selfless passivity and spiritual yielding. Submitting to men is not the same as submitting to God. In fact, we may need to learn to assert our true selves before we can really yield on deeper levels. Denying our desires, or not taking the time to explore them, means wearing the false face of the passive female. Surrendering to whatever comes along—boyfriend, employer, social expectations—is not the same as "letting go and letting God."

To return to the image of clay on the potter's wheel, clay must have a certain consistency before it can be formed into a vessel. If it is too wet, too pliable, it will not hold its shape; it will bend too easily and quickly collapse. On the other hand, if clay is too dry, it will resist change and will remain stuck in a rocky ball. If God is the potter and we are the clay, then perhaps our responsibility rests in refining our spiritual consistency—discovering if we are too wet or too dry, kneading out any hidden air bubbles, forming ourselves, not into an end product, but into material the potter can use. Preparation is a crucial step in ceramic art, and apprentice potters sometimes spend years learning to wedge clay into the right consistency before they are allowed to make a single pot. Likewise we must take seriously the work of preparing our own inner material, making it strong but pliable. By making ready the clay, we become cocreators with the potter.

Self-help books are useful only to the extent that they encourage us to do this inner work. In some ways, psychologist-authors are in a role similar to priests, ministers, or rabbis. We go to them looking for answers to life's most difficult questions. They can either give us pat, easy answers, or they can challenge us to face the questions ourselves. Like any teachers, they are most helpful when they prompt us to look within and take responsibility for our own searches and struggles. This means first learning who we are and who we are meant to be. It means admitting our fears and facing them. It means frankly acknowledging which parts of our lives are in our control and which parts are not.

In my own journey, I have found a healthy perspective among Quakers, also known as Friends. Quakers believe there is that of God in every person, so each of us has the potential for direct communication with the Divine. This belief leads to a trust of one's inner voice, rather than relying on outside authorities to instruct us how to live. Quakers recognize that God is also transcendent, greater than human understanding. Keeping these two aspects of the Divine in tension means honoring the self and our own experience while also acknowledging that we can never fully understand or control the great universe in which we live.

Depending on our experience, we may feel more comfortable with one of these aspects of the Divine. Sherry

Ruth Anderson and Patricia Hopkins suggest in *The Feminine Face of God* that for many women the spiritual challenge is to discover the God within and learn to trust her. For many men, on the other hand, the challenge is to admit that they are not in control and learn to yield. Although I believe there is some truth to these generalizations, the differences between people involve more than just gender. Race, class, and religious upbringing may also affect our sense of self in relation to God. Some of us are like dry clay that refuses to yield whereas others are as mushy as mud. Some may need to learn humility and surrender, but others may need to learn to trust their own truths. Although most of us are primarily challenged in one of these directions, we may contain both tendencies, facing different challenges in different situations.

Being active and being passive, trusting oneself and trusting God, come together in what Quakers call "following a leading." If we believe we are being led to a certain action, we can test that leading by being patient with it, knowing that true calls get stronger over time, whereas whims tend to fade. We can also test a leading by acting, taking steps to explore the possibilities. If it is an authentic leading, Quakers say the "way will open" despite obstacles.

For example, a few years ago, I felt led to become a resident student at Pendle Hill. As soon as I read the catalog—filled with photos of old stone buildings and sunstruck trees, with course titles like Faith and Feminism, and The Spiritual Basis of Our Work in the World—I knew I was meant to live in this community. My meager savings were a pittance compared with the tuition, but I felt sure the money would appear from somewhere. It did, after I requested assistance from three different sources. My persistence in looking for funding was my way of being true to my leading, but then I had to wait and let Providence open the way. One small private fund, established specifically to support people who feel led by the Spirit, offered me three times the amount I requested, allowing me to study at Pendle Hill an extra term. The letter that made this offer explained, "If it is right for you to be there, the money will be found."

Trusting that the way will open is part of trusting life's abundance, but the balance between waiting and acting can be tricky. The way is unlikely to open if I don't do anything, and sometimes I may have to overcome several obstacles before the way opens. If I wait for God to do all the work, I am not really following my call. Yet, too many obstacles might be a sign that this is not meant to be. Knowing how to read the signs, when to give up and when to persevere, is a challenging aspect of discernment.

This is true of testing a leading toward marriage. If we say we are open to the possibility of romantic love and then stay home hiding our light under a bushel, are we really giving God room to work? On the other hand, if we are scoping out men every time we go to the Laundromat, are we really waiting with trust? I believe it depends on our attitude. God works through all kinds of means, including blind dates and classified ads. What is important is the spirit with which we approach the process. Are we acting out of fear and desperation? Or are we acting out of openness and trust? Are we trying to catch a partner through manipulative tactics? Or are we opening ourselves to the possibility of love and intimacy? Or, as often is the case, are our motivations mixed?

Social conditioning may make it easier for heterosexual women to wait, given the ingrained expectation that men should make the first move. However, this assumption can make the balance between waiting and acting more difficult for lesbians and men. I've heard lesbians joke that two women can be in love with each other for years and never know it because neither one wants to make the first move. Likewise, I've heard men complain that they are still expected to take the risk of rejection, both in calling a woman for a first date and in making a marriage proposal. In discerning the balance between acting and waiting, we may also need to examine our internalized gender stereotypes.

Thirty-seven and never married, Larry would like to start a family if he found the right partner. The executive director of a grassroots organization, Larry likes strong, independent women and enjoys it when women ask him out, though he notes that the gender roles seems to be hardening as he gets older. "I definitely feel that the initiative is very much on me," he says, giving the example of a colleague who recently asked Larry if he'd go on a blind date with her friend and then gave him the woman's phone number, rather than the other way around. "That's both a privilege and a burden," he observes. "I maintain control. I can call when it's a good time for me, but it also feels burdensome."

An even bigger issue for Larry is how much effort to make once a relationship begins. "The process of my growing up and becoming more mature has meant becoming more aware of what's involved in intimacy. A big question for me is, How much is chemistry and how much is work? How much do I invent and how much do I discover a relationship?" Larry has done a lot of work to explore his own emotions and internal contradictions, including therapy and extensive journal writing. After the end of a serious long-term relationship that ultimately did not lead to marriage, Larry feels humbled by the mystery of relationships. "The older I get, the more I feel I don't know anything," he says. "I've been hurt so much. I've just come to accept being more open and attempting to be more aware. That also means realizing that I don't know anything."

Shedding our assumptions and attempting to be more open and aware is difficult. It requires an effort more challenging than searching the classifieds or the singles bars. Like Larry, Fiona says she is trying to be more open and aware, including being sensitive to how her own insecurities can block potential intimacy. A young Englishwoman who prizes her independence and yet longs for partnership, Fiona states, "I'm a great believer in fate. I always felt that you shouldn't have to do anything, that you will just meet your partner. I think, though, I've got it wrong, and you do have to put some effort into it. You won't necessarily find the right person by seeking them out, but you do have to be alert to recognizing that somebody might be right for you when you meet them, which a lot of the time I'm not. Partly it's lack of self-confidence and never believing that somebody could possibly find me attractive. Therefore, to try to pursue them would be a lost cause because they'd just laugh at me." Fiona, who is attractive and fun to be with, recognizes that her insecurity often makes her act unfriendly when meeting potential partners.

"I'm twenty-eight now," she states, observing that her biological clock is pushing her to rethink her approach to relationships. Because Fiona has endometriosis, a disease that can impair women's fertility, doctors have encouraged her to try to get pregnant as soon as possible. Although Fiona would like to marry and have children, she does not feel panicked yet by the threat of infertility. Still, she acknowledges, "It's about time I pull myself together and be a bit more aware of things going on, even basic things, recognizing that somebody actually does like me and it's worthwhile just speaking to them. I've decided to be a lot more positive and try to be open without being desperate."

Living in the tension between openness and desperation can be painful. Even if we are open to possibilities, we still have to wait for those possibilities to appear. It is far easier to close ourselves off and say, "I'm too busy for a relationship now anyway," even when we don't mean it. The path of desperate searching is equally tempting. It is *difficult* to sit in the midst of our longing, acknowledging it, and then letting it go.

I remember an afternoon class at Pendle Hill. The teacher and his wife were speaking about how marriage and parenthood had fostered their spiritual growth and made them each more whole. They talked with enthusiasm, and with obvious love for each other, as if marriage was a new wonder they had discovered and which everyone ought to try. After an hour and a half, we took a short break. As most people headed for the coffee, I noticed my friend Lorene, still glued to her seat, tears streaming down her face. A few of us gathered around her to ask what was wrong.

"They keep talking about how wonderful it is to have a partner," she cried with exasperation, "but what do you do if you don't have one? I want the kind of growth they're talking about, but I can't do it alone." I sighed and shifted uncomfortably. I knew those feelings all too well: loneliness, sadness, helplessness, impatience, jealousy, frustration. Lorene is a lesbian, so she was waiting for a woman, not a man, but that made no difference. Our feelings of frustrated desire were the same.

To say "Wait" to a tear-soaked friend seems callous, though it is the answer I have come to believe. I do not mean wait at home for the phone to ring. Wait actively, living fully in the present rather than in some utopian, imagined future. Wait like the caterpillar who knows something important is happening within the cocoon. Wait like the mustard seed, resting beneath the soil. Wait like yeast.

LIVING IN THE PRESENT

Waiting is more difficult when we assume what's happening now is less important than what's coming in the future. A germinating seed or pupating caterpillar is not exciting to watch, although the unhurried transformation within is miraculous. Neither tree nor butterfly could develop without the waiting, yet we human beings often try to skip pupation and launch prematurely into action. A platonic friendship, a disappointing romance, or a period of celibacy could all be important opportunities for growth that we forgo when we focus on where we want to be rather than on where we are. A key to active waiting is living as though *this* moment counts.

Living in the present moment is a central theme of Zen Buddhism which teaches mindfulness in daily life. When we eat, we focus on eating, rather than thinking about what we will do after dinner. When we walk, we focus on walking, rather than wondering what will happen when we reach our destination. Being mindful of every moment keeps us in the being mode rather than the having mode. It keeps our attention on loving rather than looking for a person to give us love. Mindfulness practice, which can be extremely difficult, can also be a great aid to discernment. By becoming aware of the distractions in our usually cluttered minds, we come to understand our inner conflicts and hidden motivations more honestly. By sifting through these competing voices, we make space for the voice of the Spirit to sound more clearly.

Living in the present means appreciating life as it is right now rather than staking our happiness on some future, imagined husband. Making a home for ourselves may be one expression of this, creating a place worth living in rather than just a pit stop. I read of one woman who was reluctant to buy a new stereo because she thought, "What if I meet a guy I want to live with and he already has a stereo?" In contrast, I know a woman in her early thirties who decided to buy a house alone instead of waiting for the partner she hopes to find someday. For her, this move symbolized a choice to live now rather than put her life on pause until she found Mr. Right.

Facing the couch in Betsy's living room hangs a poster with the words of William Shakespeare, "To thy own self be true." Betsy loves living alone, and the fact that she has decorated her apartment to her own tastes is an important statement about her comfort with being single. Betsy notes, "There are many things in my life that diffuse the alienation of being a single woman who's almost thirty-eight years old." She describes her immediate family, especially her twin sister, as well as nieces, nephews, in-laws, and friends. "I have people whom I can call every day, people who know me very well, people who love me unconditionally," says Betsy. "I'm an extremely fortunate person."

When we focus on the life we are living, rather than some future, imagined life, we become more aware of the many gifts we've already been given. Gratitude is a natural result of mindfulness. Even if our support system is not as strong as Betsy's, there are always reasons for gratitude. Counting our blessings every evening is a valuable spiritual practice that provides a daily reminder of life's abundance.

gratitude & thankfulness

When single, we may be especially grateful for platonic friendships. After breaking off her engagement with Ben, thirty-one-year-old Amy began building a strong circle of friends, something she had never done before. "I always used to isolate myself with that one guy, and we did everything together. Then when we broke up, I was left there standing alone. So friends are the most important thing to me now." She adds, "For once, I'm not even going to try to make a relationship happen. If it happens, great, but I'm not checking out every guy. I'm just not *looking*, I guess."

Whether we are single intentionally or by default, a period of celibacy may help us to learn to love without the expectations that often muddy romantic relationships. For Sharon, learning to trust in love's abundance was an important part of her spiritual growth. She says a four-year period when she chose to be single helped her to develop this trust. "During the time that I took to be with myself, I had so much more affection and love for my community of friends," says Sharon. "It would flow so freely in an incredible way. It was unencumbered. It didn't have any sexual connotations. It was just really loving affection." Sharon describes these friendships as lifelong, committed relationships. "Something quite wonderful happened during that time. I was celibate for those four years and loved big, loved really big." Sharon says that this experience of loving friendship now helps her to enter romantic partnership from a place of abundance rather than scarcity.

I have also learned a great deal about loving from my platonic friendships. It is easier to let go of expectations with a friend: to see the person before me, instead of what I hope they are; to appreciate fully what they give me today instead of what they may bring me tomorrow. In friendship it is easier to love a person without trying to possess them. When my romance with Kevin ended, I tried to practice this type of loving, valuing relationships in my life for what they were, living in the present rather than the future.

During this time, I became friends with a Roman Catholic priest named Tom who was on sabbatical at Pendle Hill. I told Tom about my relationship dilemmas and the ideas that were sparked by my discovery of the courtship manuals. As our friendship grew, he shared his struggles about whether to continue in the priesthood after fifteen years of service. He still felt called to work with poor people, as he had done in the central city of Milwaukee, but he questioned whether God meant for him to continue living alone, without a wife and family, as the church required. Although he had spent a lot of time in silent prayer—including a retreat where he heard a voice tell him "It's over"—Tom wanted to be certain it was really God's voice he was hearing. I had never met anyone so sincerely searching for God's guidance. I was moved by his integrity and faith. I pledged to support him in whatever decision he made.

By the end of Tom's ten-week term at Pendle Hill, my feelings were confused, and I began to wonder if our friendship would turn romantic if he were to leave the priesthood. He returned to Milwaukee to continue his discernment, and I moved to the Endless Mountains of Pennsylvania to write this book. We continued to correspond, sharing thoughts and feelings about the struggles in our lives. My writing helped me admit my desire to marry. I also admitted, to myself and eventually to Tom, that I was attracted to him, though I didn't want this to put pressure on our friendship. He was still in deep turmoil and had conflicting responses to my honestly. He was flattered but wanted to be sure he was genuinely being called out of the priesthood by God.

We both wanted to continue our friendship and agreed to be careful not to project future fantasies or hopes onto it.

This experience of friendship was challenging for both of us. I consciously tried to value our relationship for what it was without developing expectations of something more. As I wrote about fear and letting go, I recognized how much I was struggling with these issues myself. I didn't want to imitate the manipulations in the courtship manuals, yet I could feel myself trying to play it cool, calculating my words to Tom, wanting to appear impartial to his dilemmas. I sent him a quote by the Roman Catholic priest Henri Nouwen on the joys of celibacy, secretly knowing it would press Tom's sore spot, forcing him to write back a letter of rebuttal. I recognized the manipulations in myself, confessed them, and wrote furiously in my journal, hoping it would transform my heart. I truly wanted to be loving, supportive of whatever decision he made, but I knew I wasn't really impartial. I tried to fake letting go of my wants.

I finally did ungrasp my fingers after Tom sent me a cassette recording saying that he needed a break from our communication. He had reached a point where he needed to face his decision alone and would not be writing for a while. The small note enclosed with the tape had a brief message which in my alarm I interpreted to mean, "Thanks for everything. Good-bye forever." I was crushed. Over our five-month friendship, Tom had become important to me, and I feared that my desire for a romantic relationship had scared away a good friend. I resisted the temptation to write back a sweet note saying, "It's okay. Take all the space you need," and instead focused on my own need for discernment.

I knew I needed to "let go and let God" and decided a ritual might help. I gathered together Tom's letters and looked over his small, distinctive handwriting. The fact that I had kept every note and card, reading them again and again, showed I was not treating this like an ordinary friendship. I walked out to the spot where we burned our paper trash and lit a fire. I tossed in the letters, one by one, praying for the ability to let go of my expectations. Standing over the burning trash barrel, my back against a biting March wind, I knew I had to let go of the friendship, too. I had to let him say good-bye.

I was also honest with myself. In the past I would have pretended that I didn't care that much, that it wasn't such a big deal. I would have consoled myself with a list of his faults and the probability that we were incompatible anyway. This time I let myself feel the sadness and disappointment, the anxiety and the pain, as well as compassion for his pain and struggle. I recognized that sending that tape was at least as hard as receiving it, and I cried for him and what he was going through as much as for myself. I prayed, as I had in the preceding months, telling God that I thought I wanted to marry Tom, but even more than that, I wanted us each to do what was right. I prayed for the strength to let go so that we could hear clearly where we were being led. And then I had to wait.

The waiting was filled with writing, exploring the issues I was facing and trying to make sense of them. It was not an empty passive waiting. It was a time of looking within, learning to see myself more clearly and loving myself as I was. It was also a time of hope. Soon after the last snow melted, hosta buds began to poke their first tender sprouts through the soil. I felt like the land, still bare from winter, but knowing that something hidden was taking root. Using the ancient metaphor of natural growth I wrote the following.

Tending human relationships is like growing a garden. First I must prepare the soil, clearing the weeds and making compost from the relationships and experiences of the past. An old egg shell or moldy orange peel can look like garbage, but it contains the nutrients that will feed the new life that is to come. I must take the garbage of my life, give it the time it needs to transform into compost, and with loving hands turn it back into the earth.

I can till the soil, furrow the ground. I can even plant seeds and water them. But then I have to wait. I do not have the power to make a seed spurt forth and take root. That is God's work. Some seeds grow and others don't, and despite the vast gains of modern science, the whole process is still fundamentally mysterious. I can read gardening books and follow their instructions diligently, but the most I can do is create a climate favorable for miracles. I cannot make miracles happen.

I want to be a gardener of love, receiving the seeds that are sent to me and planting them with faith. I will water those seeds, fertilize them with my past, and always try to pull the weeds up by their roots. And I will wait, being grateful for whatever grows there. Such a garden will surely be full of surprises, including flowers and vegetables of varying shapes and colors and an abundance of smells and bugs. And if in the midst of this plot, there grows a plant that becomes taller and stronger than the rest, and if in the passage of time it appears that this plant is able to bear fruit, I will try to wait until the season is ripe before I pick it.

commodity, advantage, benefit

CHAPTER FIVE

Love in Bloom

To grow love, rather than buy it, we must become patient. A commodity can be selected and purchased in a minute, but any living thing requires time to reach maturity. A peach picked prematurely is bitter. Wheat harvested too soon makes poor bread. Likewise, a relationship hastily harvested may be unripe. To apply discernment to intimate relationships, we must learn to respect love's delicate timing. This applies to the first moments of meeting someone as well as to the growth of intimacy and commitment.

LOVE AT FIRST SIGHT

Four years ago, my friend Laura invited me over to dinner to meet the new man in her life, a dashing French artist named Philippe. They answered the door joined at the hip and could barely separate to set the table. In the course of the evening, I managed to get a few minutes alone with

Laura, who told me of their magical meeting on a city bus. "Philippe's visa expires at the end of the year," she said. "So we might get married a little sooner than we would have. But, oh Eileen, I have never been so happy!"

"Wow," I said, mind racing to catch up with this new development. "How long have you known each other?"

"It's amazing," she said, gazing at some point out in space. "I feel our love can't be measured in temporal terms."

"How long, Laura?" I asked sternly.

"Two weeks," she answered with an embarrassed smile.

Laura and Philippe never married, but Philippe did squander a good portion of the money Laura had saved for graduate school. More important, he squandered her trust, which has been harder to replace than the money.

I empathize with Laura's story because I see her so clearly in myself. At twenty-three, I met the man of my dreams pulling out of Albuquerque, New Mexico, on an Amtrak train. By the time we chugged into Flagstaff, Arizona, I was head over heels, and the feelings appeared to be mutual. I was certain this was *it*. All the signs were there: a serendipitous meeting, an instant connection, total infatuation. But if we were destined to be together, the guy spoiled God's plan. When he stopped calling after a few months, my faith in love was wounded as much as my pride.

The Hebrew word, *bashert* (or *basherta,* if it's a woman) means "the one God has fated for you." In English the term *soul mate* conveys the sense of a preordained spiritual connection. These words remind us that partnership is a sacred matter and that the best matches are made in heaven. But what if the guy on the train was my *bashert?* Am I destined to eternal loneliness because he exercised free will? Not the way I see it. I believe God is a matchmaker, but that doesn't mean God is rigid, unable to adapt to human mistakes. I once heard a monk say, "God gives us opportunities, but if we don't take them, God gives us other opportunities." Seen this way, the promise that God helps people get together can help us let go of our anxious searching. Rather than wondering if each new person we meet is *the one*, we can approach each new encounter willing to let God surprise us.

Today I no longer expect God's plan for me to resemble a cheesy Hollywood romance. Attraction that comes with lightning speed could be a sign from heaven, but not necessarily. I know people with great relationships who felt instantly bonded and others for whom love grew slowly, barely noticed. However quick the connection, discerning how to act takes time. Does strong attraction necessarily mean two people belong together? Does belonging together necessarily mean lifelong commitment? I grew up with the romantic myth that sudden attraction signaled destiny, lifelong love. Today I believe it takes time and patience to discern the form a relationship should take.

Some people do feel an instant connection when they meet their future spouse. For example, while on a business trip to England, Cheryl had a chance encounter that led her to meet William. Now married several years, Cheryl and William say that on the night they met they both secretly had a feeling that "this was it," even though they were living on different continents at the time. Although not everyone experiences love this way, many people do have a sense of destiny at work or a strong intuition about a relationship's future.

Our intuition may also act as a warning. Renee, who considers her intuition a source of sacred guidance, recalls meeting a man at a wedding and discussing how the bride and groom had decided to marry. "I wanted to say to this guy, 'There are things you know. For instance, I know I could never marry you.' But I didn't say that because it would have been a rude thing to say to someone you had just met." Renee laughs, explaining that she later became involved with this man, and he did ask her to marry him. "Maybe that's why that intuition was there right from the beginning," she speculates. "I don't think you can really know a person on a first date or a first meeting," she states, "but I think you can get real intuition or insight before you're biased by anything they've told you about them-selves. Sometimes you forget as you go along, and then you realize that first moment was a real knowing of certain things."

Although I believe such knowing can be valuable, there is a danger in expecting to know a relationship's future in-stantly. A rush to judge may come from impatience or inse-curity rather than real intuition. For example, I used to immediately judge and categorize any new man I met as (a) potential friend, (b) potential lover, (c) potential husband, or (d) none of the above. I believed I could recognize ro-mantic potential in the first lightning bolt of eye contact. I now blame Hollywood for this foolishness. As a girl, I mem-orized the scores to countless romantic musicals and would stand on my bed, belting out songs that described love at first sight. From *South Pacific* to *West Side Story*, the message was the same. I learned that true love was unmistakable and instantaneous and that any feeling short of temporary in-sanity wasn't *really* love.

This image of romantic love is still popular and com-pelling. The 1993 hit *Sleepless in Seattle* exemplifies the idea that if it's destiny, you'll *know* the first instant you meet. The film, which grossed over $126 million, parodies old-fashioned romantic classics and in the end becomes one.

The final scene, with actors Meg Ryan and Tom Hanks holding hands atop the Empire State Building, is schmaltzy enough to pull the heart strings of any cynic, including me. As I walked out of the theater, my mind was busy issuing a movie critique while my hands were still wiping the tears out of my eyes.

I cried at the end of *Sleepless in Seattle* for the same reason Meg Ryan's character in that movie cries at the end of *An Affair to Remember*; these romantic stories kindle our hope that love is more than just a deal. When Ryan's character gives up the man of her shopping list (her nice but dull fiancé) to follow her heart, the audience can't help but cheer for her. We want to believe in "magic" and "destiny." We want to believe that love ties us to something greater than ourselves. We want to trust life's mystery. We long for enchantment in our lives, and in a society that emphasizes profit and rationalism above other values, romance often seems to be the only place to find it. In a sense, movies like *Sleepless in Seattle* are an antidote to the consumer approach to love; they stir our imagination and encourage us to hope.

The danger of romantic films is that we take them too literally. We compare our own dull lives with the ones we see in technicolor and feel we have been cheated. In real life, God may send us a man, but not necessarily Tom Hanks. God may send us a sign, but not necessarily lightning. God may call us to partnership, but not necessarily "happily ever after." The miracle of finding a partner to love may be as dramatic as the Red Sea parting, or it may be as gradual as a germinating seed. When we expect all miracles to happen Hollywood style, we overlook the slow, quiet miracles happening under our noses.

In my twenties, I rejected any man who didn't instantly quicken my pulse—like Ed, a funny and compassionate peace activist whose company I greatly enjoyed. When Ed asked me out on a date, I lamented my lack of passion for such a nice guy. In fact, I was becoming attracted to Ed, but I dismissed these feelings because they had not been instantaneous and therefore (I reasoned) were not *real*. After sending him a series of mixed messages, I decided to clear things up once and for all. I put him in the "platonic friend" box and threw away the key.

Only after I hit thirty did I realize I could become physically attracted to a man gradually, as I got to know him, and that desire could grow from a spiritual or emotional connection. For me, slow-growing attraction has proven just as potent as the lightning and, over time, more trustworthy. This has been especially true with Tom. He is quiet, not at all like the charismatic extroverts who have usually won my heart. The first few weeks he was at Pendle Hill, I barely noticed him. Our meeting was not like a bolt of lightning, an electric flash of recognition. It was like a seed hidden in the soil that only shows signs of life months later.

When I met Tom, I was still sorting out my relationship with Kevin, and Tom was still a Roman Catholic priest. Our friendship was decidedly platonic, which made it easier for us to get to know each other without romantic expectations clouding our vision. He wanted to live in a poor urban neighborhood. I wanted to live in the mountains. Since we were friends, this was not a problem. We were not evaluating each other as potential partners or trying to sell ourselves. I noticed that every morning at Pendle Hill Tom carefully wiped his feet on the doormat as he came into the community meeting for worship. I noticed this because he was also late every morning. But I didn't judge his lateness or wonder, as I had with others, if marrying him would mean missing movie previews for the rest of my life. I simply ap-

preciated the thoughtfulness of this man who always remembered to wipe his feet.

It was such little considerate gestures that caught my attention. Tom sent thank-you notes for the smallest favors.
He noticed those left out of conversation and included
them. He listened to other people's pain with rare compassion. He was gentle with children, but not condescending.
Seeing the beauty of his spirit helped me notice the beauty
of his body: the laugh lines around his eyes, the strength of
his arms, the gentleness of his hands. I became attracted to
the whole of him, not body versus spirit but his entire being.
Developing a strong platonic friendship before becoming
romantically involved gave us time to work through individual issues—especially his decision to leave the priesthood—which we each needed to face alone. It also gave us
time to develop deep respect for each other.

When Tom resigned from active ministry in the priesthood several months after leaving Pendle Hill, he con-
tacted me, and we arranged to meet. When we saw each
other again, it was clear to both of us that we did want to
explore a romantic relationship, letting things develop at
their own pace. Because we were already good friends, we
did not begin by trying to sell ourselves. Instead we continued building on a relationship based on mutual acceptance.

Tom and I were fortunate to have met in the relaxed atmosphere of Pendle Hill—sharing classes, chores, and meals
in the dining hall. Often new acquaintances don't get the
chance to share a meal without labeling it a "date," a word
which, by implying romantic possibility, escalates anxiety
and expectation. In the absence of some shared community,
making even an initial acquaintance can be difficult. As a
single woman in a big city, I used to lament the large number of men visible but unreachable. In theory, the dating op-

portunities were inexhaustible—especially compared with those of my foremothers in rural Ireland—but in reality, most new men flashed across my view screen so quickly (at the bus stop or convenience store) there was no chance to get to know them. For those living without the web of social connections typical of smaller communities—where the cute guy at the store probably went to school with your brother, and his mother plays bingo with your neighbor— it's no wonder a lightning bolt or a guerrilla dating tactic seems necessary to break through the initial boundaries of strangers.

The key is to let go of our preconceived ideas about how love is supposed to happen and accept that there is no standard blueprint for romance. The door to our heart may feel a sudden, urgent pounding or a gentle, insistent rap. We may open the door to find someone not at all like we expected. Listening to the stories of people I interviewed, I was struck by the variety of ways romantic love can arrive— quickly, slowly, smoothly, turbulently. One couple (now married thirty-two years) became engaged the day after they met. Another initially disliked each other and only fell in love several months later. For some couples, attraction was instant, but working out whether they should marry took years. In other cases, one person knew long before the other. I've concluded that, yes, you'll know when it's right—but you won't necessarily know the first time your eyes meet.

PHANTOM LOVERS

When Gene Kelly dances with his umbrella in the movie *Singin' in the Rain*, he captures the joyous, irrational, irreverent feeling of new infatuation. Kelly jumps gleefully in puddles, sings to the sky, and at the end of the song, gives away his umbrella to a passing stranger. An onlooking policeman thinks he's nuts. This nutty feeling is exactly what we love about infatuation; it allows us to discard logic and express the playful, passionate parts of ourselves that are usually kept in check. Infatuation is exhilarating, energizing, distracting, befuddling. It colors our perceptions and shifts our priorities. It makes the world seem new and magical. It makes the most petulant partner seem perfect.

In the first flush of infatuation, my expectations can run as rampant as my hormones. My mind fast-forwards through the movie script to the happy Hollywood ending, where lovers set off together, forever young, fit, and clear skinned. It's an attractive fantasy. The *Sleepless in Seattle* model of love ends when the lovers first hold hands. We never see the part where they struggle over which city to live in or how to share closet space. We don't know if they have compatible values or similar ideas about child raising. Their love is frozen in the last frame of the film, before passing through the fire of real relationship.

In *We: Understanding the Psychology of Romantic Love*, Jungian psychologist Robert A. Johnson argues that modern Western culture expects more of partnership than previous cultures. We expect marital love to contain the bliss of mystical experience along with the nitty-grittiness of daily life. We expect our mate to represent a perfect divine image, but we also expect him or her to take out the garbage, change the diapers, and balance the checkbook. The conflict between these images leads to disappointment, and we begin to wonder if "true love" might be elsewhere. Johnson urges us to let go of our romantic fantasies and seek "stirring-the-oatmeal love," finding the sacred in the humble and ordinary. He concludes, "Ultimately, the only enduring relationships will be between couples who consent to see each other as ordinary, imperfect people and who love each other without illusion and without <u>inflated expectations</u>."

Inflated expectations can lead to painful disappointment. Renee recalls her childhood belief that she and the man of her dreams would be "in continuous telepathic rapport. He would know what I thought and what I wanted without my ever having to put it into words," she laughs. "I assumed we'd agree on every matter." These expectations were shattered by her first boyfriend, Evan, whose background and personality were very different from Renee's. Although Renee's intuition had led her to choose Evan over another man, that didn't mean that Evan fit her idealized image. She recalls writing a poem about her "phantom lover," the imaginary perfect man who blocked her ability to fully enjoy Evan: "The idea came to me one day while Evan was washing up at the sink, and I was looking at his really beautiful body and his physical presence. I thought, 'How could this person who is present and alive be somehow less real to me than this fantasy that I have?' I spent a lot of time when I wasn't with Evan imagining how our relationship could be more perfect. But I once said to myself that imagining how our relationship could be more perfect was not nearly as much fun as actually relating to him, even though he wasn't perfect." Renee realized that being with a person who had his own way of seeing and doing things enriched her life. "But even so, it didn't stop me from being angry that he wasn't the way I thought he should be, or that he wasn't the perfect fantasy lover."

My own phantom lover is a composite from television, movies, and advertisements. He has the mind of Carl Sagan, the courage of Captain Kirk, the wit of Mork from Ork, and the rippling biceps of a Calvin Klein model. He has been stiff competition for the real men in my life who, unlike this phantom, always seem to have faults. I remember my first kiss in eleventh grade and my horror at feeling the boy slobbering on my face like an excited puppy. He was a far cry from the urbane suitor I had imagined would win my first kiss. It took me fifteen years of dating to realize that real men were more interesting than my phantom. I had been looking for a modern Apollo instead of a real human being whose particular imperfections would help me to grow as a lover.

Carl Jung argued that we all unconsciously carry archetypal images of the opposite sex which we project onto the real men or women in our lives. According to Jung's theory, my phantom springs from collective and personal experiences of masculinity; pop culture figures, like Captain Kirk or Mork from Ork, are merely modern representations of older, more universal images of the warrior and the fool. To grow toward wholeness, Jung asserted, individuals must discover within themselves qualities thought to belong to the opposite sex and integrate them into their own personalities. The marriage of the feminine and masculine within each individual, which Jung believed was facilitated by a conscious marriage relationship, is an important step toward becoming one's true self.

We may find that our checklist really describes the person *we* want to be (successful, athletic, creative), and looking for those qualities in a partner distracts us from developing them ourselves. Paige notes, "I find attractive in other people what I wish I was but don't feel I am. Then that develops into problems because I want that person's being it to fill my need to be it too, and it doesn't." When Paige, a small-framed activist, first met her tall, rugged partner, she admired his athletic ability and wanted to accompany him skiing and mountain climbing. But when they went, she couldn't keep up, felt inferior, and had a miserable time. This caused friction so they both stopped doing the fun things that had attracted Paige to him originally. The tension eventually eased when Paige worked on developing her own athletic abilities, making her feel better about herself and allowing her to keep up on their outings. Her experience is a reminder that we can't expect a partner to complete us. At best, partnership can motivate us to develop ourselves so that we have a stronger self to bring to the team.

Jane and Fran exemplify how this process can take place in a lesbian relationship. A professional therapist, Fran notes that her relationship with Jane has nurtured both the "masculine" and "feminine" sides of her personality. "Being two women together allows us to use other parts of ourselves that we wouldn't use in a heterosexual relationship," states Fran, pointing to household projects they might have left to their husbands, if they'd had any. At the same time, Jane says she feels like more of a woman in this relationship than she did when she was married to a man, partly because she feels so safe sharing her emotions. Their willingness to talk about emotions and to "process" what's happening between them also helps to make their relationship more conscious.

Knowing that a partner will not fill in our missing pieces can help us let go of our quest for our fantasy lover. We can acknowledge what we hope for, then put away our checklist and open ourselves to a real human being. Each person includes strengths and weaknesses interwoven into a tapestry more beautiful and mysterious than the sum of its parts. As long as we measure a person by a list of their assets, we miss the beauty and mystery of the tapestry.

Twenty-four-year-old Jodi recalls, "When I was seventeen, it was all going to be perfect, like I thought my parents' relationship was. Then when they got divorced I realized how unrealistic that was." Working through her parents' divorce was a painful struggle for Jodi, but from it she learned that partners need to communicate to make a relationship work. Now back together with her high school sweetheart, Bruce, she comments, "We're now more realistic about accepting our own faults and accepting each other's. When you're seventeen, you still think you're going to grow up to be perfect, and now we're realizing we're who we are and beginning to accept that." While going to college and then working in different states, Jodi and Bruce dated off and on. Through their periods of separation, they discovered that they truly loved each other. "That was the important thing," says Jodi, "not whether our political views necessarily jibed completely or whether we matched each other's exact criteria for this and that. It was just that we loved each other so much. When we weren't going out, we worried about each other."

Loving a real human being, imperfections and all, is not the same as "settling," another idea that grows out of the consumer concept of love. We settle when we feel we are bargaining from a position of weakness, like when our childbearing years are passing and our market value is depreciating. We may shorten our shopping list to one basic requirement: willing to marry me. We may call this realism. But settling leads to disappointment just as surely as expecting perfection. In fact, they are two sides of the same coin. Both approaches come from the fantasy that there is such a thing as a perfect partner; the only difference is in whether we expect to be winners or losers. Compromising is not the same as settling. Settling means accepting a relationship that does not help us grow as a lover rather than facing the pain of singleness. Compromising means accepting a partner who, despite outrageously human flaws, helps us to love God, self, and others more fully.

It's not just that seeking someone perfect is unrealistic and, therefore, likely to lead to disappointment. Seeking someone perfect means trying to avoid the challenge and real potential of a relationship. It's our rough edges, and those of our lover, that create the friction that polishes. A partner's faults can help us learn forgiveness. A partner's wounds can help us learn sensitivity. A partner's ability to point out our imperfections can help us grow. I remember Kevin telling me that I talked more than I listened. The comment stung as only a criticism from a lover can, but because I loved him, I listened: to the comment, then increasingly to the people around me. It is this type of growth that makes a relationship exciting after the first flush of infatuation fades.

Although Nancy hoped to marry and have children before her biological clock struck midnight, most of the men she dated in her twenties were long-distance lovers whom she saw only during contrived weekend rendezvous in settings where the phone never rang and mundane concerns were forgotten. Rick, whom she met while carpooling to a conference, was different. Rick lived near Nancy, challenging her to fit him into her everyday life. They answered phone calls when they were together and talked about their struggles as high school teachers. Nancy says her relationship with Rick "wasn't a fantasy world"; it was much more healthy. But the day-to-day reality wasn't always easy. Nancy recalls, "Fighting was really hard for me in the beginning." Nancy grew up in a family where showing anger was taboo, so she was horrified when, after she and Rick moved in together, they began arguing over housekeeping chores and control of the television remote. "There were plenty of times early on when we would fight about something, and I would be convinced the relationship was over," she says. The process of facing and resolving such issues helped Nancy learn to express both anger and forgiveness.

Nancy recalls, "I had always thought that I would get into a relationship, and it would just be perfect, and everything would be wonderful. And somewhere in that year I realized that making a relationship work took effort. It didn't just happen. Everything wasn't magic, and we weren't perfectly suited to each other. There were things that needed to be worked out, and there were compromises. And there are things we still haven't worked out after five years." Nancy says that realizing that she could be furious at Rick and still love him "made me realize it was the right relationship. To some extent, being able to fight made me realize that."

The German poet Rainer Maria Rilke wrote that "once the realization is accepted that even between the *closest* human beings infinite distances continue to exist, a wonderful living side by side can grow up, if they succeed in loving the distance between them which makes it possible for each to see the other whole and against a wide sky!" Loving the distance between us means accepting conflict in a relationship and letting it teach us. It means accepting that our beloved is an ordinary imperfect human being, more mysterious and interesting than a phantom. It means accepting our own vulnerabilities and risking being loved for who we really are, not the advertising image we've created. Only by getting past the advertisements and the consumer approach to love can we experience real intimacy with another person.

Opening ourselves to a real human being, we may be surprised to discover qualities we didn't realize were important.

For example, Nelson, who has been married to Marian almost fifty years, recalls that as a young man he wanted to marry a woman who played the piano. "Marian can't play the piano, and she was just the opposite of all that myth I had set up," he explains. "But that was very unimportant when I found somebody who I felt comfortable with. I wasn't afraid to talk to her." Other people interviewed made similar comments, often pointing out that they didn't realize what was really important until they found it. Such stories remind us not to be too specific in our prayers. We may be better off letting God surprise us.

THE LOVE PLAN

We are often reluctant to let God surprise us, especially once a relationship has begun. We want "success" in romance (as in everything else), hence the popularity of books telling us how to improve communication skills and sexual techniques. Although some relationship manuals include good advice, we delude ourselves if we believe that proficiency in pop psychology can control the future of a relationship. Who can explain why one heart leaps in the presence of another? Who knows why one relationship continues to grow, despite many difficulties, and another that started smoothly fizzles after a few months? And who is to say that the romance that fizzled was a failure if it taught us a valuable lesson? Rather than trying to steer a new romance toward a preconceived destination, we might be better off stepping back and letting it lead us, waiting to see what a relationship has to teach us.

Erich Fromm pointed out that psychology—which literally means "science of the soul"—originally sprang from the desire to *"understand the human soul in the interest of making people better."* He argued that much modern psychology "has a different purpose. Its goal is not to understand the soul so that we can become *better* human beings; its goal is—to state the case crudely—to understand the soul so that we can become *more successful* human beings. We want to understand ourselves and others so that we can take the upper hand in life, so that we can manipulate others, so that we can shape ourselves in ways that will favor our own advancement."

Fromm's point is graphically illustrated by *How to Make a Man Fall in Love with You*, which asserts that new psychological findings about human behavior are "the long-missing link in the mystery of love." The book's "Love Plan" involves carefully observing a man's gestures and then mirroring them back to him. "Does he tap his fingers? Does he jiggle his foot?" the author asks. "If he does, you should unobtrusively and subtly pick up his motion." The same goes for his breathing rhythm and speaking style. These techniques "will rivet his attention on you. You will make him feel as if you are his soul mate." Author Tracy Cabot boasts, "Even the most elusive lover will be powerless under your spell."

This behaviorist pop psychology is antithetical to the "science of the soul" offered by Thomas Moore in *Soul Mates: Honoring the Mysteries of Love and Relationship*. A psychologist with religious and poetic sensibilities, Moore writes, "The heart is a mystery—not a puzzle that can't be solved, but a mystery in the religious sense: unfathomable, beyond manipulation, showing traces of the finger of God at work." To enjoy more soulful relationships, Moore argues, we need less analysis and more imagination, more respect for magic. Emphasizing the futility of treating love like a

futurity - uselessness

project, Moore writes, "All intimate relationships require some degree of magic, because magic, not reason and will, accomplishes what the soul needs."

The contrast between Moore's reverence and the courtship manuals' scheming illustrates fundamentally different approaches to relationships. Moore is concerned with nurturing the soul, whereas the courtship manuals are interested in achievement, possession, success. If my goal is to possess another person, to put him under my spell, manipulative tactics may not seem so bad. The ends justify the means. But if my goal is to be a loving person, to nurture my beloved's soul, as well as my own, the thought of jiggling my foot in time to his seems ridiculous at best. Even if these tactics did get his attention, attention does not equal love.

Although, like Moore, I believe love is a gift and a grace, beyond human control, that doesn't mean I have always practiced what I preach. At times I've tried to steer the love boat by acting in ways I thought men wanted me to act. I became a blues fan while courting a guy who loved the blues. I acted interested in architecture while dating an architect. The biggest difference between my behavior and the "Love Plan" was that I mirrored these men unconsciously rather than deliberately. There have been times when my conscious mind thought I was being loving, only to realize later how I had tried to make myself appear more generous than I really was. This has been particularly true in terms of patience. I have sometimes acted more patient than I felt, so my attempts to accelerate a relationship were subversive rather than overt. Whether unconscious or deliberate, however, our attempts to hurry love can be terminal.

IMPATIENCE

A passage from the novel *Zorba the Greek* by Nikos Kazantzakis aptly describes the danger of trying to rush a miracle. The narrator recalls discovering a cocoon in the bark of a tree just as a butterfly was slowly beginning to emerge. To speed the butterfly's appearance, he eagerly breathed on the cocoon to warm it:

> I shall never forget my horror when I saw how its wings were folded back and crumpled.... It needed to be hatched out patiently and the unfolding of the wings should be a gradual process in the sun. Now it was too late. My breath had forced the butterfly to appear, all crumpled, before its time. It struggled desperately and, a few seconds later, died in the palm of my hand.

The narrator describes the butterfly's body as "the greatest weight I have on my conscience" and concludes: "We should not hurry, we should not be impatient, but we should confidently obey the eternal rhythm."

Tom sent me this quote from *Zorba* a few months after we both left Pendle Hill. He was deep in his struggle over whether or not to leave the priesthood while, several hundred miles away, I wondered what type of relationship we would have if he did leave. I had told him I was attracted to him—not, I reasoned, to initiate a romance while he was in the priesthood or to pressure him to leave but instead to find out if the attraction was mutual. If it was, I was willing to wait for him to discern his life's direction. Tom sent the *Zorba* quote with the tape explaining that he needed to break off communication with me and face his decision alone. Although he intended the quote to describe his own need to wait, it slapped me in the face with my own impatience. I realized I had spoken out of insecurity rather than concern for him. Telling him how I felt about him while he was trying to patiently wait for God's guidance had only made his process more painful. This realization helped me stop focusing on his decision and instead focus on the letting go and trusting that was crucial to my spiritual growth. Ironically, pulling away from each other and refocusing on God freed each of us to come together a few months later when the time was ripe.

This experience prompted me to consider different ways impatience can injure a relationship. I've observed three common ones: verbal impatience, sexual impatience, and commitment impatience. Verbal impatience is the impulse to speak one's feelings prematurely, as I did with Tom. I am an advocate of honesty but not unthoughtful, unbridled honesty where we selfishly unburden our hearts only to burden another. I think of a single female friend who was distraught because a married man had confessed his attraction to her. He said he wasn't trying to start anything; he just wanted her to know how he felt. "Why does he want me to know?" she wondered anxiously. My friend had enjoyed the company of this man and his wife, but now she felt wary and uncomfortable. His confession had stirred her feelings of loneliness and desire, but he was unaware of the impact of his words.

Silencing our feelings could be manipulative, defensive, or loving, depending on our motivation. If we keep quiet to play "hard to get," our silence may be a tactic. If we keep quiet to protect ourselves from the risk of rejection, our silence may be a defense. But if we keep quiet because we have not yet discerned a call to speak, our silence may be a loving protection of both hearts, allowing time to discern what should be said. Writing about spiritual discernment, Roman Catholic bishop Robert F. Morneau suggests, "A basic guideline in terms of time and waiting is the following: 'act on your clarities.'" Discernment needs time, and we may have to wait before the right course becomes clear. "Once that happens," says Morneau, "hesitation becomes sinful."

I usually err on the side of impatience rather than hesitation. More than once, I have blurted out my feelings for a man in the name of honesty, figuring I wouldn't want to be with a guy who was easily scared off anyway. In retrospect I wonder if my "honesty" was just a different form of manipulation, one that enabled me to claim the moral high ground because I was "just being honest." Real honesty includes being honest with ourselves about our motives. Are we trying to assess which strategy (speech or silence) will get us what we want? Or are we asking what is called for in this moment, trying to find the path which nurtures both self and others? The challenge of discernment is to act as we feel called to without trying to generate a specific response in another person.

Similar questions relate to sexual impatience, though with higher stakes. Sex can be life giving or it can be deadly. It can be loving or selfish. It can grow out of deep intimacy or be sold as a commodity. Because of its transformative power, our society is deeply conflicted about sex. For some, it is the ultimate symbol of freedom and creativity. For others, it is the symbol of dangerous individualism and irresponsibility. Most of us probably contain a mixture of these views, their relative strength influenced by experience, religious background, and generation.

The lives of the women in this book span the century, and their stories reflect the dangers of both puritanism and promiscuity. "In my day, we rushed down the aisle because we were horny!" exclaims one woman in her seventies, arguing that the prohibition against sex before marriage encouraged her peers to marry in haste, often repenting at leisure. In contrast, thirty-one-year-old Amy first had sex at age fourteen and learned to expect sex within the first few weeks of a relationship. "Especially as a woman, you can definitely lose yourself once you've had sex," says Amy, recalling that after sex with a new boyfriend, she has often focused her life around his.

Breaking off her engagement with Ben prompted Amy to reflect on her relationship history. She now feels taking sex too lightly has hurt her, and she has decided to enter sexual relationships more slowly in the future, keeping her grounding and developing friendship and mutual respect first. I've heard Amy's experience echoed by both women and men who, in the wake of the sexual revolution, have decided to go more slowly than they had in the past. Some feel that establishing friendship and trust before becoming sexually active makes a relationship more likely to last. Others say sex clouds their vision, making it difficult to see another person realistically. One friend of mine asserts that for her sex is such a powerful emotional experience that she feels "swept away" and loses her capacity for discernment.

One problem may be that our culture has developed an all or nothing view of sex. In her book *Promiscuities: The Secret Struggle for Womanhood*, author Naomi Wolfe argues that in the past three decades, Americans—particularly young Americans—have lost the art of gradually moving around the "bases." Rather than a slow progression of intimacy, which allows a sexual relationship to develop along with trust and friendship, sexual activity is often equated with intercourse, with an expectation that a new couple will "go all the way" early in their relationship. Wolfe asserts, and I agree, that it is safer to explore a relationship's sexual potential gradually. I also believe that sexual gradualism makes it easier for us to take the time to discern our intentions for the relationship and discover if our passion stems from lust or love.

Seeing sex as a sacred gift, and discerning when and how this gift should be enjoyed, is more difficult than following rigid rules or no rules, but it allows for more complexity in our moral decisions. Instead of defending our "right" to sexual pleasure without love (as one *Cosmopolitan* article puts it), I defend our right to be fully loving people and to discern for ourselves how our love can best be expressed. As with any discernment, timing can be crucial. Sex is like an unfolding butterfly—beautiful and delicate. Our pleasure-seeking culture provides the hot breath that can draw the creature out too quickly. But rigid morality that keeps the butterfly locked in its chrysalis is just as deadly.

Again, knowing our own motives is important. If we believe sex only reaches its spiritual potential in a context of commitment, waiting to have sex may be motivated by love. On the other hand, withholding or withdrawing sex in order to generate a marriage proposal is a time-tested feminine tactic. With this motivation, waiting is manipulative rather than moral. We use his sexual impatience to satisfy our commitment impatience.

There is a difference between desire for commitment and impatience for commitment. The desire for a mutually committed relationship may be healthy and loving; it may even be a sign that we are called to the vocation of marriage. Commitment impatience, on the other hand, is the urge to pick the fruit before it is ripe. It comes from seeing marriage as the goal of a relationship and wanting to reach that goal as soon as possible. Commitment impatience is usually fueled by fear: fear of the biological clock, fear of rejection, fear of being alone. It may be amplified by social pressure or the romantic myth that all true love lasts forever. It can take many forms: rushing to evaluate someone's partnership potential, subtly pushing for a proposal, issuing an ultimatum. In essence, commitment impatience means putting the desire to get married ahead of the desire to be a loving person.

When we are impatient for commitment, we focus on the future rather than the present. We see getting married as something to be achieved through determination and strategy rather than a gift and a grace. We focus on getting what we want rather than on knowing what is wanted of us. We see partnership as a product rather than as a process. Ironically, this focus may make it more difficult to develop a committed partnership. Several women interviewed noted that when they were impatient to get married they couldn't relax and be themselves, and the men they were dating were scared off as a result.

LOVE AS A PROCESS

If we see marriage as a goal, then dating is a means to an end. Every date brings us a step closer or diverts us from where we want to be. Every relationship that doesn't lead to marriage is a waste of time, a failure. But if we see every breakup as a failure, we may miss a relationship's true purpose. My struggles with Kevin included painful disappointment, but they ultimately helped me to listen, wait, and trust love's abundance—exactly the lessons I needed to prepare me for Tom. Even if Tom hadn't come along, those lessons would have been worth the pain. Many women interviewed shared similar experiences, showing how loss and letting go can open us to something new.

Of course, no one enters a romantic relationship for the growth experience they'll get out of the breakup, and it is normal to wonder where a new romance is headed. But when we are focused on trying to determine a relationship's future, we fail to nurture its present. Recalling her first boyfriend, Evan, Renee comments, "Instead of appreciating the relationship and enjoying it, I was continually asking myself, 'Can I marry him? Is he good enough for me?'" This constant questioning kept her from appreciating him for who he was.

Cultivating gratitude can help us to live in the present. Appreciating the grace that brought us together makes it easier to appreciate the person before us. Appreciating the gift of relationship heightens our awareness of all the gifts we have received, helping us to trust that this relationship will evolve as it is meant to and that we do not need to grasp and clutch. Being grateful for what is helps us to be less anxious about what is to come.

When beginning to consider the future of a relationship, rather than asking, "Is he good enough for me?" we might ask, "What is this relationship asking of me?" or "How can I nurture its growth?" Without trying to control the outcome, there are things we can do to nurture a relationship. Walking in the woods, taking dance classes, writing love letters, sharing dreams, baking bread, eating by candlelight—the possibilities are endless. Worshiping together may have special meaning. During our courtship, Tom and I were part of a small Sunday worship group that included prayer, shared reflection, and homemade brunch. This weekly gathering nurtured us individually and as a couple, strengthening our desire to help each other grow toward God.

Supporting each individual's growth is one way to nurture a relationship. Although Lynn considered herself an agnostic at the time she met her husband, Walter, she was intrigued by his interest in dreams and reincarnation. "I always had a spiritual life," Lynn explains. "I just was very alienated from Christianity. I wouldn't have been happy marrying someone who was an agnostic or an atheist because I needed to be nurtured into a deeper faith." Walter, who died ten years after they married, nurtured Lynn's faith by encouraging her own seeking. Lynn says that's what their relationship was all about: "We had basic, deep, fundamental longings and searchings, and respect for that kind of thing. We could go off in our separate directions and have distance in the relationship because the center core was based on something—not that we'd go to the ball game together, not that we loved grocery shopping together—but we enjoyed being friends with each other, talking to each other. He'd cut out an article and say, 'I think this would interest you.' So he was a teacher and a lover, and we both were growing."

Accepting the differences between their beliefs also helped them grow. Lynn was suspicious of Christianity, observing all the violence in the world that had been committed in Christ's name. She recalls, "When my husband asked if he could put his walnut cross up in our house, I said, 'Not where I can see it very often.'" After Walter's death, Lynn gave the cross to a Mennonite minister to sell at a garage sale fund-raiser. In time, Lynn came to find meaning in the story of Jesus, and when she discovered that the minister had never sold the large walnut cross, she shyly asked for it back. Although Lynn still recoils from the harm that has been done in the name of Christianity, she came to appreciate the symbol of the cross in her own time and her own way.

Differences—from religious ideas to housekeeping styles—begin to emerge during any courtship. People can respond to those differences with openness and curiosity, or they can flee from the challenges they present. Discussing a difficult issue could bring a couple closer or it could tear them apart, and for some that may seem too big a risk. Acknowledging the individuality of another means accepting that person's free will, separate and distinct from our own. This means risking pain and rejection, but it also means opening to a more profound intimacy. By seeking to know and nurture our partner, even if it means risking his or her loss, we experience what it means to truly love another.

Loving another while loving ourselves can be particularly challenging for women and men trying to understand each other across the gender divide. Amid changing gender roles and backlash politics, seemingly trivial issues may be laden with implications about identity and respect. For example, I dated one guy who always wanted to be the driver on our dates. His car was newer and nicer, so at first I didn't mind, but after a few months I became uncomfortable, feeling it was symbolic of his assumptions about gender roles. When I raised the issue, he got defensive, which put me on the lookout for other evidence of his ingrained sexism. In contrast, the first time I went somewhere with Tom, I insisted on driving and said I thought women and men should take turns behind the wheel. Tom didn't seem to mind, a response that took the potency out of the issue for me. Once I knew he was flexible about gender roles, questions such as who drove or who paid for dinner lost their symbolism. Once I knew he respected my strength, I no longer felt I had to prove it all the time.

Today many heterosexual couples want an equal partnership but are unsure how to create one given the depth of our gender socialization and, often, the depth of our pain. I find it helpful to remember that when it comes to creating equal relationships between the sexes, we are all slogging through new and muddy terrain, with few markers before us. Women complain that men don't "get it." Men aren't sure what "it" is, but they feel unfairly blamed for it. Women don't want to be perceived as passive or helpless, yet they still often expect men to take the risk when it comes to initiating a date or a marriage proposal. Broaching such issues during a relationship's development can be an important part of coming to understand each other's experience. To do this, however, we must be willing to risk conflict and misunderstanding.

Women are conditioned to be the peacemakers, even at the expense of their true selves. Several courtship manuals—focused only on the goal of marriage—warn women to avoid all conflict that might keep them from throwing the bridal bouquet. But this creates a false peace, one that is not loving. If one of us is sad or angry about some aspect of our relationship, deflecting this feeling may also thwart the possibility of real growth and change. Denying our lover's unpleasant feelings means denying who he is, refusing to see him as a whole human being. The same applies to our own difficult emotions. Like the avoidance of quiet and solitude, avoiding conflict keeps us from reaching our full humanity, our desperation and brokenness, as well as our creativity and inspiration.

The process of deepening a relationship may even require times of painful separation, as Leigh Ann and John experi-

enced. Leigh Ann, who is now thirty-six, recalls meeting
John two years ago while both were in the Peace Corps in
Guinea-Bissau, West Africa. "He kind of scared me," she
laughs, describing John's long stringy hair and ripped blue
jeans. "We use to laugh about being Mary Tyler Moore and
Jim Morrison." Under his scruffy surface, Leigh Ann discovered a sensitive, intelligent man who shared her vision
of education. Working with him on curriculum development, Leigh Ann's respect and affection for John began to
grow. "I felt this little thing pop up inside, and I said, 'Can
this be what I think it is?' "

Leigh Ann and John soon acknowledged their mutual attraction and began three months of incredible bliss where
everything they did together seemed unbelievably wonderful. Their differences complemented each other in their education work. They moved in together and talked about
having a baby. Leigh Ann says she knew within days that
the essence of their relationship was permanent partnership, but figuring out the shape that would take took time
and struggle. Leigh Ann recalls, "John would go through
these periods of thinking, 'Oh my God. What am I giving
up?' " She notes that being six years older, she had spent
more years living alone than John had. "He hadn't lived
with his freedom long enough to see the other side of it,"
she says.

They began to discover the ways in which their differences chafed. Leigh Ann says, "I love cities and reading
books, and John loves walking around in the mountains."
John would be happy living in a small village in Guinea-
Bissau; Leigh Ann missed her American friends, indoor
plumbing, and the *New York Times*. John had also enjoyed
sexual experimentation and was unsure about committing
to a woman. "So then comes all the ways that a partnership

can limit one," notes Leigh Ann. "How can the two of us both be happy? If Leigh Ann can't be happy staying in Guinea-Bissau and John can't be happy leaving it, there's not much of a compromise." They decided to separate, a decision that was devastating for Leigh Ann. She says she had a "very firm feeling inside that somehow we're supposed to be together. So, that was pretty rough for a very long time." Working at the same school and passing each other in the village were excruciating for Leigh Ann, who decided to speak to him only when absolutely necessary. Her voice grows quiet as she describes that time: "I think I came really, really, really close to dying."

When the next school year began, John left her a note saying he'd like to come talk about work issues. Leigh Ann knew it was really an effort to ease the tension between them. She was cautious as they began to work together again and anxious about her ambiguous feelings. "I'd have these visions of being gloriously, hugely pregnant with John, and I'm thinking, 'Wait! That's not the conversation we just had. We were just talking about getting funding for the workbooks. So why are these thoughts and feelings still coming?' That made me very uneasy," she explains.

A few weeks later, John told her how visiting a neighboring country during the semester break had opened him to the possibility of leaving Guinea-Bissau and had made him think about connections and being connected. "What are you connected to?" Leigh Ann asked. "And just out of his mouth comes, 'You.' He never intended to say it," she recalls. John later said that during the time they were separated, he felt like he was walking around with a veil or curtain. He could see, but things were fuzzy. Then, when those words came out of his mouth and he recognized his deep connection to Leigh Ann, it was like this curtain opened and everything was clear. As they began to rethink their relationship, it became clear to both of them that they wanted to spend their lives together.

Leigh Ann struggles to describe what this process meant: "It's sort of like deciding that what you want is the truth. You want what is true. And it's a question of being open. You can't make something happen or manipulate it." Leigh Ann recalls that while they were apart, a friend of hers was planning to visit a psychic medium, and Leigh Ann considered going too. "I thought, 'Now what is it you really want her to tell you anyway? Some magic potion to get John back?' Finally, I realized, 'No. I just want her to tell me what's true.' I think realizing that, and holding firm to that, has made a lot of things come clear. 'Cause you'll know when it's true. Confusion can still happen, and you've got to pull yourself back to say, 'What is true?' "

Today, Leigh Ann and John live together in the United States. They have exchanged rings to represent their life-long commitment to each other, but they are still discussing whether or not they want to have a public wedding ceremony. Leigh Ann explains, "To me it's a story of there being this core, cosmic connection between the two of us that has always been so clear, and it's all these earthly trappings that have made it hard or confusing at times." She adds, "I'm sure confusion is still to come."

The real mystery of a relationship is revealed through the passage of cycles and seasons. We could not claim to know an oak tree after only seeing its full summer leaves. The depth of autumn color, the bareness of winter branches, and the freshness of spring buds are equally essential parts of the oak. We must watch the slow but daily changes in a tree before we can claim to know it as a friend. But we live in a society that is quickly forgetting the lessons of nature. Patience, an essential quality for a farmer, is not highly valued in our high-speed, high-tech world. We expect everything to come with overnight delivery and a money back guarantee, even love.

Love's seed is a gift from God, but it is up to us to tend it with care and patience. Too much water can drown it. Too much sun can scorch it. Too much fertilizer can burn its roots. Waiting is essential to gardening—waiting for the right time to thin the crop or prune the shrub. Waiting for the fruit to ripen before it is picked. Like a hatching butterfly or a blooming flower, love cannot be rushed.

CHAPTER SIX

Approaching Commitment

$\mathscr{W}$ith the package concept of love, we see marriage as a business deal: I'll meet your needs if you meet mine. Closing the deal is the goal of most courtship manuals, which focus on "negotiating a sound engagement" and "getting to 'I do.'" With this mind-set, however, wedding vows are just a business contract. Once the contract is broken, it is no longer binding. Like an efficient manager, we are entitled to fire an employee who is not doing his job. This is very different from the old-fashioned vow to love "for better, for worse; for richer, for poorer; in sickness and in health." A shrewd manager would never accept such conditions. Her business contract would include an escape clause in the event of poverty, sickness, or other unforeseen difficulties.

When we see love as a process, rather than as a product, commitment is not a goal; it is a special way of loving. It is not a guarantee of what we will receive; it is a promise of what we will give. Commitment brings a new safety to a relationship, but it also brings new risk. When we hear a call to commit ourselves to another, that call is not a triumph; it is a gift, a grace, and a challenge.

THE CHALLENGE OF COMMITMENT

Many writers, both theologians and psychologists, argue that commitment is necessary for the potential of marriage to be fulfilled. When we are in a casual relationship, it is easy to walk away from the wrestling mat. We may leave a relationship rather than work through the difficult times. Or we may suppress issues in the relationship, fearing that conflict will tear us apart. Although marriage doesn't come with any guarantees, if two partners enter it sincerely vowing to stick with each other in good times and in bad, their promises can create the safety necessary for them to reveal their true selves. Years of shared living create the opportunity for this unfolding to occur.

The value of commitment is most clear during difficult times. Bridgette and Peter met during college and lived together for five years before they married. A few years later, shortly after their first child was born, Peter had what Bridgette calls "a quasi affair" with a coworker. "That shook us up," recalls Bridgette, "but it also defined what marriage was for us." Through the pain of Peter telling her about it and a year of therapy afterward, they realized what their marriage meant to them and how much attention and effort a marriage required. "We learned a lot of wonderful tools and checks," says Bridgette. "We realized that these low times will come, and that temptations will be there, and that our choice is that we want an intact family, for our children and for ourselves. We really came out of that experience a much stronger couple and truly committed to working things through. So in a lot of respects, I think we were very fortunate to have that experience young, rather than ten years later or something. We also had very good help in dealing with it."

Bridgette says their faith in God helped them through "in the process of forgiveness and learning to trust again." For Peter, she observes, "At that point, it was his wants versus something that was more difficult. It was something that just feels good and feels fun right now versus staying with what feels hard. And the commitment to stay with what feels hard I think in a lot of respects comes from having strong family roots and a faith community who do just that."

Staying together required effort, honesty, and flexibility on the part of both partners. Bridgette did not ignore Peter's infidelity or pretend it didn't hurt her. Peter did not deny it or act like things were fine at home. Instead, they were honest and wrestled with each other through the difficulty. "Whammies can happen in your relationships," says Bridgette. "They probably happen to most of us, and many of us make that choice to stay together and to make things better."

Committed to a life of celibacy, Kathryn argues that it is in fidelity to our own paths that single and married people can relate to each other. Kathryn asked, "What does it mean to make a vow to marry someone? Do you just leave when there's the first bit of trouble? Or is that in fact the way God is working in your life? And you hang in there. I don't mean if you're being abused you should stay in your marriage and all that, but oftentimes I think we leave too quickly before we really see how God is working in this situation. If that is truly your vocation, you're supposed to hang in there. Just like the person in the monastery, however many years later, starts to question, 'Wow, do I really want to wash raisins all day and pray?' So, 'Do I really want to do this batch of diapers? And here his socks are on the floor again, and there's another meat loaf.' That sort of thing. How is God working in that?"

Trusting that God is working through the difficulties of marriage can help us to be faithful. For example, Annette, who has been married to a Protestant minister for over thirty-four years, feels that much of her own spiritual growth came through intense conflicts in her marriage. "When I was in my young forties, I came to see what I had never seen before, and wouldn't have acknowledged even if somebody had told me. I came to see that my husband was at the center of my life rather than God." Prior to that insight, Annette believed God was at the center of her life, so this realization was deeply disturbing. She states, "Although my husband is very religious, that was a very difficult thing to undo because he had gotten accustomed to being at the center of my life."

Annette began to bring marital problems to the surface, despite her husband's resistance. "By following what seemed to be the promptings of the Spirit, and believing in the sanctity of marriage, and believing that God was with us, I just persevered, all the time totally uncertain as to what was going to happen. I alienated my husband for a few years. He said things like, 'Our marriage is dead, so we should get divorced,' while I always held on to the concept that without death, you can't have resurrection.

"Well, that's how it turned out," she states. "We had resurrection. As a result, we're both much more whole people." Annette explains that working through the conflict freed them from old emotional and psychological baggage, such as her husband's jealousy. Today, Annette's career brings her all over the country, often working with men. "I do things now that I know twenty years ago would have driven him up the wall. But somehow in the course of all that, he developed incredible trust." Today, Annette finds it hard to imagine how either of them could have grown so much without the struggle.

It took years of painful conflict for Annette and her husband to learn this new way of loving, but both partners grew as a result. Their willingness to work through the tough times shows how friction within a committed relationship can polish each partner. But there is a difference between friction that polishes and friction that bruises. This distinction is illustrated by Irene, whom I happened to interview on the same day as Annette. Both women grew up with marriage as the assumed norm. Both centered their lives around their husbands, and both eventually challenged this arrangement. However, Annette found "resurrection" within marriage, whereas Irene describes her divorce as "a kind of resurrection."

"I think for my generation it was pretty much assumed that a woman's life was orbited around a man's life," states Irene, who married in 1959, one year before Annette. Soft-spoken, with her gray hair pulled back in a bun, Irene describes how she spent seventeen years attempting to fit into her husband's affluent world, increasingly losing touch with her own values and needs. "I spent years thinking, 'Well, maybe if I do it this way, or maybe if I change that, it will all work out all right.'" When she finally began to assert her own priorities, her husband reacted viciously. Irene says of her divorce, "It was, in a way, trying to get my soul back."

Irene's husband was vehemently antireligious. After leaving him she began to explore meditation and then prayer, finding new friends who supported this growth. As she grew to understand who she really was, outside of the roles she had tried to play, her life was gradually reconfigured so that it centered around God rather than a man. Irene describes this process as typical of spiritual formation. "There is a psychological dimension to finding one's own focal point and insisting on moving around that," states Irene. "That is where religion and psychology lie so close in terms of what is a true self and what is a false self." Over the years, as Irene has come to know herself more deeply, she has found she is suited to a life of solitude, spending much of her time reading and writing about spiritual issues.

The primary difference between Annette's and Irene's stories is not the ending, but the beginning. Their original motivations for marrying were different. From the outset, Annette felt marriage was a spiritual path and believed God was part of their married life. In contrast, Irene made a deal to fulfill social expectations. She got children, nice clothes, and trips to Europe; he got a wife to run his home and throw dinner parties for his law partners. "I became converted to a kind of status symbol," observes Irene. As a status symbol, there was no room for Irene to grow without breaking the contract. Her husband would not accept changes in her that would challenge him to change, too. Annette's husband, on the other hand, was eventually able to grow and change with his wife. Their marriage was ultimately flexible enough to stretch without breaking.

If we appreciate that growth can come through struggle, we may be less likely to leave a relationship when it becomes challenging. Yet not all difficulties are growth producing, as Irene's story illustrates. Although Annette experienced "resurrection" by working through the struggles of her marriage, Irene described her divorce as a "resurrection." Discerning when to stay and when to leave may require special strength and patience, especially when we have been taught that divorce is always wrong.

A member of a Pentecostal church, Carolyn says she believes in having one marriage for life, though she is now going through her second divorce. When she was twenty-two, already with two daughters, Carolyn decided to marry the father of her children. Divorced by thirty, she married another man just about the time she was coming back to the church. Both times, Carolyn says, a little voice inside had warned her that it was a mistake, but both times she ignored her internal guidance, thinking marriage would give her and her children security. Now firmly rooted in the church, Carolyn believes that God has guided her to leave a destructive marriage, despite the deep shame associated with divorce in her community. "I didn't just decide overnight," explains Carolyn. "It took me many years to come to this point. I gave him so many chances. The last five years I've been giving him chances to get himself together, and he's gotten worse."

In addition to his frequent drunkenness and his disregard for her religion, Carolyn explains that her husband committed adultery repeatedly. It was by a strange coincidence that she found out about his cheating and the possibility that one of his mistresses might be HIV positive. Carolyn credits God with letting her know what was going on and protecting her from the virus. "It was hard for me, getting the divorce," she says, "but every time I start to doubt myself and I pray, this little voice come back to me and say, 'If he wasn't for me when I married him in eighty-five, he's not for me today. So why am I holding on to something that will never be for me?' That gives me confidence. I think God is letting me know that I'm doing the right thing." Carolyn's pastor does not believe in divorce under any circumstances, although the wider umbrella of Pentecostal churches has in recent years recognized adultery as the only valid reason for divorce. "There's a conflict there," says Carolyn, "but I'm listening to the big umbrella and my own heart, too. I have to go with my own conscience and my own heart. I can't let my pastor dictate my life."

Distinguishing God's guidance from the guidance of one's religion can be painful, though for Carolyn believing that her marriage was never God's will makes seeking divorce a bit easier. She never saw her marriage as a vocation. Instead she sees it as a mistake that she is now correcting. In such situations, divorce may be the path that enables both people to grow as lovers. But what if we deliberately practiced discernment, felt led to marry, then later feel called in a different direction? Does this mean our original discernment was faulty? Is it possible for a vocation to change? These are difficult questions, with no easy answers. Especially when children are involved, finding the path that honors God, self, and others challenges us to hold other people's needs at least equal with our own. We may need to thoroughly scrutinize our own motivations before we can find a solution that cuts all ways.

In *Called: New Thinking on Christian Vocation*, M. Basil Pennington points out that a vocation is not always lifelong. A person who for a portion of his or her life feels called to a certain kind of work may later be led in another direction. For some, this change may evolve naturally. A woman whose primary vocation is motherhood may feel a new call when her children are grown. For others, a change may require painful decision making, even the breaking of vows. Pennington argues that such a change may be a valid call that is necessary for the person's continued growth toward God.

As a Franciscan sister, Michelle feels her vows of poverty and chastity are freeing rather than limiting, enabling her to love more broadly. Although she has wholeheartedly given herself to her calling, Michelle notes that her primary commitment is to God, not to her community or the church. "The calling comes from God," she explains when asked if a vocation can change. "Who am I to say, 'Okay God, you can't ask me to do anything else now'? Right now I can't conceive of what that would be for me personally, but I think it can happen. And that can be a real painful thing for people to discern through, asking, 'Is this *really* of God?'"

The question "Is this really of God?" is at the heart of discernment. We can be pulled by many voices, not all of them divinely inspired. Boredom, fear, insecurity, and selfishness are all powerful and loud. In approaching the possibility of marriage or divorce, discernment challenges us to look at our motives and our resistances and ask, "Is this really of God?"

IS THIS REALLY OF GOD?

It may be impossible to answer this question with certainty. If we want to marry, how do we know if this desire comes from our inner guide or the voice of convention? How do we know if marriage is the best way we can grow as a lover? How do we know if someone is the right partner for us? There is no foolproof method for answering these questions, but as suggested in *Listening Hearts: Discerning Call in Community*, "Humility, grounded in self-knowledge, helps us to avoid the distortions of both inordinate self-confidence and exaggerated self-doubt."

Peace and clarity are signs of true discernment, but what if we do not yet feel peace? We may need to work through a hodgepodge of issues and emotions before clarity comes. The fears discussed in chapter 3—such as fear of singleness or marriage, loneliness, and the biological clock—may resurface, needing to be revisited. Or the proximity of a commitment may raise new fears we have yet to face. For example, we may fear being among the majority of new marriages that end in divorce. I have listened to friends pour out their pain as unions begun in hope end in bitterness. I have watched children divide their possessions between two houses while their parents argue over where they'll spend Thanksgiving. When Tom and I began discussing the possibility of marriage, knowing so many good people who had divorced added some humility to my discernment process.

In Quaker tradition, people often write a list of queries to facilitate their discernment. For example, to discern if we are being called to marriage, we might ask: Do I love my partner for who he or she is, or for what he or she gives me? When I am with my partner, do I feel more truly myself, or do I hide my true self? Does this relationship bring us both closer to the Divine, or does it act as a substitute? Does our relationship bear fruit for those around us? Do I need to commit myself to this relationship to fulfill its purpose? Is there another call that I will turn away from if I commit myself to this relationship? Such questions cannot be answered through rational analysis alone. Instead we need to quiet our mind to hear whether a yes emerges from our heart.

Lynn says she always had a spiritual life, although she was suspicious of organized religion, particularly Christianity. When she married the first time in her twenties, she made the decision "methodically, carefully, and logically," but the marriage was a painful disappointment. Several years later, when she married her second husband, Walter, who had cancer at the time, Lynn was "more willing to risk and take a leap of faith." Lynn's father had died from cancer when Lynn was nine, and her mother was appalled that she would marry a man who might be dying. Lynn recalls, "My friends said, 'You're marrying somebody who has cancer, is older, doesn't have a job. There must be something that attracts you there.' And I realized that it's not rational the way you come to clarity about major decisions."

When making a decision that seems illogical to family and friends, we may be especially prone to self-doubt. If those around us are relying on logic, rather than discernment, our inner guidance might not make sense to them. Lynn's mother, who had been a young widow, wanted to spare her daughter the same grief, not realizing that Lynn's marriage to Walter would actually bring her healing. Walter did die ten years after they married, from an illness unrelated to the cancer, but the time they shared together fostered their growth and helped Lynn regain the trust of life she had lost when her father died. In choosing to marry Walter, Lynn had trusted her own sense of what was right even though it didn't make sense to people around her.

Socially, marriage joins families as well as individuals, making an individual's choice of marriage partner a potentially emotional issue for the whole family. To risk conflict with our parents by selecting someone of the "wrong" race, religion, or gender can be extremely painful and confusing. We may need the strength to endure their disapproval if we want to follow our inner guidance. On the other hand, we also need to be certain we are not using our choice of partner for rebellion or revenge. For example, Elizabeth recalls that her Southern Baptist mother was "not thrilled" when

Elizabeth met her future husband. "He was a Yankee, God forbid," she laughs, "and Catholic, God forbid again!" As their relationship became more serious over the next three years, part of Elizabeth enjoyed rebelling against her mother, though another part of her was afraid to consider marrying Dave because of her mother's opposition. It took time for her to sort through these emotions and feel confident that marrying him was the right thing to do.

Relying on our inner voice does not mean we should discard the observations of people we trust. Sometimes others see us more clearly than we see ourselves. A valued friend may be able to sense when we have unloving motives we would rather not admit or when our behavior fits an unhealthy pattern. Those close to us may also be able to see our partner with a distance and perspective we lack when we are newly in love. The perspective of a confidant who is skilled at discernment may be particularly helpful in confirming or challenging the rightness of a decision. Saint Teresa of Avila, a well-known mystic who put great faith in her direct conversations with God, herself checked her discernment with a "confessor" and advised the sisters in her order to do the same.

Knowing how much to trust someone else's perspective, especially when it conflicts with our own, can be challenging. Even if we listen to the opinions of those close to us, even if those people are practicing spiritual discernment, no one else can directly experience our inner guidance for us. Although others can tell us if our actions seem in harmony with who we are, we may have an inner experience of knowing that no one else can truly understand. When this experience is sudden or seems irrational, it may be particularly difficult to sift through, requiring time and patience to discern if the guidance really is of God.

A dynamic artist with long, curly hair and a distinctive laugh, Zoe met George on a crowded airplane when she was twenty-seven. Their eyes met, and as Zoe describes, "I had a feeling that this was the *one*." Within a month of their meeting, they said they wanted to marry each other. "That's when the power struggle began," recalls Zoe. "We struggled over where I fit in his life and where he fit in my life." Zoe and George decided they were not yet ready to marry, and it was another two years before they officially became engaged. By that time, Zoe's family and friends had heard many stories about George's temper, and virtually everyone close to her expressed concerns about the frequency of their arguments.

Zoe had her own fears. She had made many sacrifices for her art and was fiercely protective of her independence. "I was afraid of logistical things," she recalls, "like not having my own apartment, not living by myself, not being in control of all my money—not that I had much." She also had fears that were specific to their relationship. George had a history of not respecting her boundaries, and despite two years of couples counseling, Zoe was unsure if she could believe his promise that he would support her artistic career. She knew she was terrified, but she couldn't tell whether she was afraid of commitment, a fear she wanted to overcome, or whether she was afraid to commit to George. "I didn't have enough life experience to know which it was," she explains in hindsight.

For months, Zoe prayed for guidance. She felt a clear calling to help George care for his two boys from a previous marriage, but she didn't feel peace or clarity about the other issues in their relationship. In the end, she decided to take a leap of faith and dealt with her fear by focusing on the wedding plans. Soon after their beautiful June wedding,

George became physically abusive, and during their two-and-a-half-year marriage, he systematically broke every promise he had made to her. Now recently divorced, Zoe says she should have paid greater attention to the prewedding fears that were warning her of real danger. She also acknowledges that her friends and family were right to be concerned. But despite the pain of the past few years, Zoe is certain she had a positive impact on George's boys and feels she was right to stay in the marriage until she was able to arrange for them to get professional help. "I have grown so much from this experience," she says, explaining that she is a stronger, more creative, and more compassionate person than she was before her marriage. She has tapped inner resources she didn't know she had and is blossoming spiritually and artistically as a result.

Zoe's story raises several difficult questions. What was it that led Zoe to marry George despite her own fear and the concern of those close to her? If her fear was a warning from her inner voice, then what was the voice that told her that George was "the one" the first time they met? And what of the call she felt to care for the boys? Zoe feels there was truth in all the voices, though she is still trying to understand the contradiction. One possibility, she feels, is that God gave her and George an opportunity for a good marriage, but George exercised free will by hitting her, destroying that opportunity along with her trust. One of the many lessons for her has been to listen to every voice inside her until she reaches a place of stillness. When she made the decision to leave her marriage, she experienced a sense of peace and certainty that she never felt about her decision to marry. Now that she knows what real peace feels like, she knows what to wait for in future discernment.

THE UNCONSCIOUS MIND

Modern psychology has helped us realize the power of the unconscious, and many psychologists assert that our unconscious chooses our mate rather than our conscious mind. Patricia, for example, was startled by a Freudian slip that revealed an unconscious desire. Now married to Brad for twenty-three years, Patricia recalls that five days after meeting him she was about to tell him something about love that she had been rehearsing in her head: "I opened my mouth and what came out was, 'If I'm going to marry you . . .' I got that far into the sentence and went, 'Gasp! I didn't mean that! I don't know where that came from. I don't know why I said that.' " Brad didn't appear alarmed, but he didn't say anything else about marriage . . . until a few months later when he proposed.

Although the unconscious can get our attention in a variety of ways—such as physical attraction, intuition, fantasies, and Freudian slips—dreams are among our most common encounters with the unconscious. Renee, who writes and teaches about mysticism, has studied her dreams for years. She describes the first time a dream helped her to make a decision during her junior year of college. The passion was fading in her relationship with her boyfriend, Evan, and Renee had a crush on another guy, Bart, who was also interested in her. Renee was trying to decide whether she should break up with Evan to pursue Bart. "I had this intensely erotic dream about Bart," she recalls, "but when I woke up I couldn't remember what the dream was. I just remembered this erotic feeling." Later in the day, she suddenly remembered the dream and realized that all she and Bart were doing in the dream was creating a better hamburger together. Renee laughs, "When I remembered the details of the dream, and not just the erotic feeling, I said to myself, 'What does this mean? I'm a vegetarian! Is this all we're doing? Is this the best thing that can happen with me and Bart, that we make a better hamburger together?' And I interpreted that dream to mean that the relationship with Bart would essentially be shallow, or not the kind of thing I really wanted, because it was a hamburger, and I was a vegetarian. And on the basis of that dream, I decided not to pursue a relationship with him."

How do such experiences relate to spiritual discernment? What is the connection between the unconscious and God? These are difficult but important questions. John A. Sanford, a Jungian therapist and Episcopal priest, bridges the perspectives of religion and psychology in *Dreams: God's Forgotten Language*. Citing seventy biblical passages referring to dreams and visions, Sanford asserts that the Bible is "the story of God's breakthrough into man's conscious mind via the unconscious." He suggests that "the self, the psychic center, or God within" is connected to a greater, transcendent God. A comparable view is offered by Morton T. Kelsey, another priest-therapist, who asserts that "the dream may be one of the most common avenues through which God reaches out to us." Both writers point out that dreams were a respected means of discerning God's will in the early Christian church but have been largely ignored by the church for the last several centuries.

Although dreams can be important instruments of discernment, humility and self-knowledge are especially important in dream interpretation. Because dreams are symbolic, they are easily misinterpreted by the conscious mind, which tends to put its own spin on things. In her dream about Bart, Renee might have seen the hamburger as a sign that a relationship

with Bart would be "meaty" or substantial and used this to justify dumping Evan. But her vegetarianism significantly affected the meaning of the symbol, and Renee knew herself
well enough to recognize this. Like any art, dream interpretation takes practice and patience. Since dream figures usually
represent various aspects of our own psyches, learning the language of dreams can deepen our self-awareness and hence our
discernment. Dreams are rarely directive, however. In most
cases, dreams reveal the struggles within us, leaving us to
choose the appropriate response.

In any discernment—whether we look to dreams, scripture, or silent prayer for guidance—there is a temptation to
hear what we want to hear. We may be especially tempted
to confuse wishful thinking with intuition about a relationship's future. As the authors of *Listening Hearts* comment,
"A healthy skepticism of our own motives is a sign of spiritual maturity." This does not mean paralyzing self-doubt but
simply "humility, grounded in self-knowledge." Practically
speaking, waiting before we act is one way to test our discernment. If we have heard a call correctly, our sense of
peace and clarity should last over time.

Helen laughs at herself as she recalls the years she dated,
racing against her biological clock. "Five minutes into any
relationship, I always decided that *this* was the man I was
going to marry," she confesses. "I learned just to ignore myself for the first several weeks, to enjoy the high that I got,
and to try and keep my head about me." Now married and
with an adopted son, Helen says once she got past the initial infatuation, it became very clear whether a relationship
was worth pursuing. "I learned to trust that I wasn't going to
do anything foolish and end up with somebody who I
couldn't stand to look at across the breakfast table." Because
she knew the patterns of her behavior, Helen waited to see

if her feelings lasted, following her deeper intuition not just impulsive attraction.

Like Helen, my intuitive wires have often gotten crossed in the first flush of infatuation. I have come to trust my intuition in choosing jobs, apartments, cars, and friends. But when choosing men, I have learned not to be impulsive. There have been times when I was *sure* romance was about to blossom, only to be disappointed. In retrospect, I realize that on those occasions I felt expectation but not peace. When I feel something is supposed to happen and also feel a need to make it happen, there is anxiety. I am secretly scheming how to make my intuition come true. When I am really sure, I don't feel a need to do as much. I am more patient, calm, and trusting.

Intuition about a relationship's future can serve a loving purpose if it helps us trust rather than manipulate. Now married several years with three children, Bridgette recalls meeting her husband, Peter, while they were both attending a small midwestern college. "It's totally irrational, but I did feel like this was the person," she says. "It was like I was being told, and I *knew* on this level that I was going to marry him." Bridgette had never dated much and was uninterested in a casual relationship. She says her intuition that Peter was the one helped her to be patient during the five years of their courtship. "Mostly I was okay about waiting for him to decide that he was ready," she says, explaining that she had "a lot of trust and faith" that someday they would marry. Bridgette reflects that having grown up in a religious family, she believed that God would show her whom to marry. Although she feels more comfortable with rational thinking, she wonders if "the God part of that would be the feeling of knowing."

Whether we believe our intuition comes from God or our

unconscious or both, only time, patience, and peace can confirm its rightness. When Tom and I became romantically involved, I had an unwavering intuition that this relationship would lead to marriage. This sense was deepened one night while we were staying with my mother. Wearing a flannel nightgown, I went to the living room to kiss Tom good night. He was writing in his journal on my mother's couch, the couch my grandfather had died on, the couch where I had watched TV with my father late at night as a young girl, the couch where relatives sat when they came to visit. He looked so at home, I thought. I gave him a kiss and a hug, wished him sweet dreams, and went back to the bedroom I was sharing with my mother. Climbing between the sheets of my childhood bed, I put my head on the pillow and felt a deep sense of peace. With sureness, I knew that Tom was becoming my family. I knew that I wanted to share my life with him, and I knew that I would.

This intuition came to me several months before Tom reached the same point, but because the intuition was accompanied by a sense of peace I didn't feel I needed to do anything to convince him. There were difficult moments as we sought to make our discernment mutual, but I believed that if I was being led to marry Tom, then he would feel the same leading when the time was right. I simply had to wait.

MUTUAL DISCERNMENT

Commitment impatience can have a poisonous effect on the growth of a marriage. A person pressured into making a commitment may feel his or her resentment swell years later in the midst of an argument over the checkbook. The person who did the pressuring might harbor doubts that his or her partner ever really wanted to marry. To create a mutual, loving relationship, our decision making must also be mutual and loving. The ends and the means are inseparable.

So how does discernment work between two people? What if one partner feels called to marriage before the other? How do we trust our own internal guidance while respecting someone else's? One model comes from the Quaker practice of group discernment. Community business is decided during a "meeting for worship for the conduct of business" based on the belief that there is divine guidance available, and if each person seeks to be open to the Spirit, we will eventually be able to find unity on even the stickiest issues. "Eventually" is an important word here, since it can often take years of discussion and struggle before unity is found. Through trust, listening, patience, and a good clerk to facilitate the process, Quakers believe people can put their individual egos and agendas aside to hear a greater truth.

Recognizing the fallibility of individual discernment, Quakers often use group discernment to corroborate an individual's clearness. A person who feels a leading may ask for a "clearness committee," a small group of discerners who through prayerful listening and supportive questioning help the person sort out whether the leading is really of God. Two individuals in an intimate relationship can also practice discernment with each other. There may be times when this flows easily, when what is called for is clear to both people at the same time, but there may also be times when they need help reaching clarity. For this reason, meeting with a "clearness committee" is part of the process of seeking marriage "under the care of" a Quaker meeting. In some cases, the rightness of the marriage is clear to everyone, and the committee's questions serve as marriage preparation. In other cases, the clearness committee provides a space to seriously question whether or not the couple should wed. What happens when two people, each listening for God's call, hear conflicting answers?

"There's a Quaker answer," replies Rebecca. "You wait. And I think there's a lot of wisdom in that process. Even Quakers today place so much emphasis on the individual, I'm not sure we're really willing to practice." Rebecca has learned patience and mutuality through her vocation to motherhood, but she recalls that prior to her marriage, she was very impatient. When Rebecca and Stuart were preparing to marry under the care of a Quaker meeting, their clearness committee had concerns about their readiness and asked them to wait. "I allowed it to push me into my desperate place," she says. "I wanted this so badly I had to have it, and I think Stuart, in a sense, acquiesced." Rebecca believes that her impatience, as well as Stuart's reluctance to acknowledge honestly his reservations, had negative consequences for their marriage. "Waiting is part of mutuality," she says, "and speaking honestly is the other part of mutuality. Every one of those little resistances needs to be trusted, every one, just to be brought up into the open waiting, without needing to do anything at first but genuinely hear them."

Hearing reservations, rather than burying them, gives us a chance to learn more about ourselves, our partner, and our relationship. We may not feel deep peace until we listen to the other voices and sift through what they have to teach us. If we trust that God is at work and that peace will come in time, we can learn to trust the process. By speaking honestly, listening nondefensively, and waiting patiently, we help create the space where God's love can reveal itself.

Hearing our partner's reservations about marriage can be

painful, however. Jean, a fifty-eight-year-old grandmother, recently married Lorene in a Quaker wedding. Jean had never had a lesbian relationship before and was as surprised as anyone when she fell in love with Lorene and wanted to marry her. Since both women were Quakers, belonging to a segment of Quakerism that supports same-sex marriages, they consciously practiced discernment, including meeting with a clearness committee. Jean recalls, "There were times along the way when she sounded doubtful, and that would be really hard for me. I think that's partly her style, and I'm learning this, but it was very hard to feel that." When asked how to deal with someone else's doubt, Jean suggests, "Take a long-term perspective and know that there are going to be low times for you and low times for the other person when you might be doubting—doubting them, or doubting yourself, or doubting everything—and those times don't feel good."

Jean observes that listening for a call to marriage is different than other discernment she's experienced. "You're so much more vulnerable," she says. "You just have to open yourself in a different way than when you make other kinds of decisions." Although Jean made herself especially vulnerable—moving from the city where she had lived for thirty-six years to marry a woman—I suspect we all feel vulnerable when opening to the possibility of partnership. We're putting our egos on the line, risking painful rejection. Jean recalls the period when she first realized she was attracted to Lorene and her terror before she told Lorene how she felt. Jean remembers a friend asking her what she was scared of: " 'Is it being a lesbian?' And I said, 'No, I'm scared she isn't going to love me.' "

This simple statement, "I'm scared she isn't going to love me," reveals one of the deepest fears we carry into relationships. At the same time we long for love and acceptance, we fear being rejected by our beloved. We may take our partner's reservations about marriage very personally, making it more difficult for him or her to acknowledge honestly all the fears that need to be worked through. For example, during their engagement, Zoe's fear of marrying George stirred up his fear of abandonment, making him cling to her all the more tightly. "He was a very persuasive and manipulative person," Zoe explains in hindsight, recalling that she was never able to get the space she needed to work through her own feelings. "A person who loves you will give you the space you need," she counsels. "If he won't give you space, that should be a clue something isn't right. But when you're caught up in it, it's hard to see that."

Even with loving motivations, giving someone space may be difficult. Nancy recalls, "I was ready to be engaged probably about eight or ten months before we actually got engaged." Although she and Rick were living together and talking about spending their whole lives together, Nancy was concerned about her biological clock and felt frustrated they were not doing anything concrete to formalize their commitment. "We had this big fight where I basically got really grumpy that he hadn't brought up marriage. We talked about it, and he said he just wasn't ready, which I took as this huge rejection. He said, 'It's not a rejection. I'm just not where you are right now. It doesn't mean I'm not headed there.' "

They let the subject rest for a few months until one night when they were doing errands at the mall. Rick told Nancy he wanted to show her something and led her into a jewelry store. Nancy recalls, "He showed me engagement rings, not because he liked their engagements rings, but just to sort of show me that the train had moved a little bit. I remember when we looked at the rings, I was just speechless, and I wouldn't even try anything on." Nancy gasps and makes a face of dread, imitating the anxiety she suddenly felt now that marriage was on the horizon. "All of a sudden, I felt like he was miles ahead of me on this engagement thing," she says. "That is typical with him. It takes him longer, but once his train gets on track, it goes very quickly. So somehow our trains got a little crisscrossed." Nancy's story is a reminder that both partners may have anxieties about marriage that need to be faced. If we focus only on our partner's reservations, we may not fully acknowledge our own.

Only by listening to our anxieties can we begin to know if they are temporary growing pains or serious warnings. If concerns persist and we do not feel led to marry a specific person, we may still feel a sense of clarity and peace about our decision. A few years ago, when she was in her late thirties, Helen struggled to discern her future with Carl, a man she deeply loved. Helen very much wanted to marry and have children, and Carl was the first man she ever seriously considered marrying. Although they greatly enjoyed each other's company, they had very different values, and Carl didn't share Helen's sense of spirituality. "We did so well together that it was hard to figure out if our very different values were that big a deal," she explains.

Eventually it became clear that values were a big deal. On a New Year's Day walk with Carl, Helen felt the words come to her clearly and strongly: "This has to be it. We can't do this." Helen says the breakup wasn't that painful for either one of them because they had reached a mutual point. "The words came to me," she recalls, "but either one of us could have said it, because we were that close to discerning where we were." With hindsight, now that they are both married to other people, Helen notes that during her relationship with Carl, she drifted away from her faith community: "It wasn't until after that relationship was over that I could see how it pulled me away from my own spirituality."

Helen's story is a reminder that no might be the answer that honors God, self, and others. Being willing to say no may be especially difficult when our partner has proposed. We may feel loved and validated, knowing someone wants to marry us. We may feel that rejecting a proposal would be cruel or unloving. We may fear this is our "last chance" before the biological clock hits midnight. Accepting our partner's no is not any easier. Because we feel so vulnerable when making this decision, we may not come to mutual clarity as smoothly as Helen and Carl. Saying no to the possibility of marriage, even when we feel clear that it is the right thing to do, may cause pain and sadness.

Mutual discernment can move quickly or slowly, with ease or with struggle. It is a process as unique as each couple, so there is no model of how to discern a call to marriage. To illustrate this, here are a few stories of mutual discernment told more fully. Although very different in some ways, each of these stories illustrates the themes of letting go, listening for divine guidance, and leaping with faith that have been explored in this book.

TOM AND PAT

Before they met, Tom and Pat had each been married and divorced. Each had grown children, and neither was interested in marrying again. Tom, a Presbyterian minister dedicated to living and working in poor, urban communities, had recently moved to a neighborhood ravaged by unemployment, drugs, and violence. Pat, who was also Presbyterian, had lived most of her life in affluent suburbs. She was attending Eastern College and focusing on improving her education.

Pat recalls her attitude when a good friend asked her if she would like to remarry: "I said, 'No Ann, I wouldn't.' I said I was married almost twenty-five years, had two children, and that was a wonderful experience, but I think God has something else planned for me. Ann said, 'Oh, yes, yes,' making a 'Yeah, sure,' face, 'but if it was a *really special* man?' And I stopped, put my hands on my hips and said, 'Ann, that man has not been made!' " Pat laughs, "So that was my attitude. When Tom and I met, even that very day, there was still never a flicker of marriage in mind."

At the time, Pat believed God was guiding her in a new direction. She went to the college chapel regularly, "really communing with God, and just pouring myself out to Him, being with Him, and very, very open." From that sense of openness to life, Pat agreed to let her friend Ann fix her up on a blind date with Tom. The two of them had immediate chemistry, and halfway through their picnic date they were leaning up against each other. Pat explains that this was very unusual behavior for her. "I am much more reserved in that way, always have been, and never assertive. But I leaned, couldn't help it. It was like a magnet!" By the end of the evening, Pat was petrified by the strength of this attraction.

"For me, it is so bound in my faith that I'm almost not sure where one thing begins and the other ends. I felt that this was meant to be, like predestination. And I don't mean that blandly, because so much goes into that, the working out, the saying yes to life. Saying yes to things instead of no changes the direction of your life," like being willing to say yes to the blind date, explains Pat. "It was not long, a matter of weeks after we met, that we knew that this was it. We just knew." Tom confirms this, recalling their second date: "I can still remember seeing Pat coming down the street, and I knew this was the lady. . . . Four months later, we got married."

The quickness of their courtship did not mean it was without struggle. Pat laughs, "My mind was saying no, no, no, but my body and everything else was saying yes, yes, yes. There was a lot of just sitting in the contradiction." Pat recalls that during their brief engagement she went to the chapel one day to pray. "Suddenly this white, paralyzing fear came over me, and I said, 'Oh, God, I'm petrified. Getting involved with this man means getting involved with his ministry. I don't know that I'm strong enough to do this. What about this love place in me that seems so fragile? It's never been touched or harmed by anything in my life.' And then I heard a voice that was not my own say to me, 'That love place is my gift to Tom through you.' And then the voice said, 'Don't worry. You'll have everything you need.' It was so clear and so certain that I relaxed."

"It's been true," adds Tom.

"It's been true every step of the way," confirms Pat.

Working together, the two have turned a closed-down church building into a vibrant community center. Their partnership has nurtured Tom and helped him to grow emotionally, while Pat has blossomed in skills and confidence through their community involvement. But she adds that even with this experience and the reassurance she heard in prayer, she still sometimes forgets to trust and becomes anxious. Then when things work out, she remembers the promise that she would have all she needed. "And I say, 'Wow, why didn't I realize that?'"

She concludes, "Ultimately it is a risk." No matter what

your discernment process, she says, "You still cannot know for sure until you test it. I had no desire to get married, so here I was acting out exactly opposite to what my mind was telling me." She felt she was being led by something very strong that she just had to trust. She pats her abdomen, explaining that she tries to let her gut inform her head, rather than the other way around. "My mind came around after a while," she explains.

JUDY AND MICHAEL

Before she met Michael, Judy had thought about ways to commit herself to God's service. She imagined becoming a nun in Mother Teresa's order, but she was not Catholic. She then seriously considered remaining celibate on her own, although friends thought she was crazy. Judy was still sorting through these issues when Michael was hired to work with her on a program that builds bridges between people of different classes and races. They were both in their twenties.

Judy recalls, "Here comes Michael the first day of work. He was real outgoing, and I wasn't. He had a lot of personality, and I had none. He just took over the office." Judy was Michael's boss, and she was afraid his outgoing confidence would completely overshadow her quiet demeanor during his eighteen-month internship. She recalls, "I went home and wrote in my journal, 'Eighteen months minus one day to go.'"

Michael agrees they got off to a bad start and says he thought Judy was a "zero." "I was arrogant enough to know who was important and who wasn't because I was planning to run the world," he says, mocking his youthful ambition.

Although he was initially unimpressed with Judy, Michael wanted to make their work relationship as productive as possible, so he suggested they have lunch together every Wednesday. "That was a very good idea," recalls Judy. "It made us talk, and we got along better because of it." Because their work involved intense weekend programs and the discussion of difficult issues, they got to see each other at different times of the day and under varied circumstances. Judy notes, "It is good for our marriage that we started out knowing all each other's bad sides, all the faults, before seeing anything good at all. It wasn't like going out with somebody and trying to impress them, and wondering if they know what you look like when you put glasses on. We didn't do that." Having to make many difficult decisions together, over the next year they developed deep mutual respect and a strong friendship.

"It was clear to me that Judy wasn't the big zero I had thought she was," Michael explains. "Then I decided that Judy was a saint in some way, which a lot of people decide after they get to know her." As his attraction to Judy grew, he recognized that neither of them were the type of people who dated casually. If he was going to pursue a relationship with her, it would be because he wanted to marry her. He laughs recalling his hesitation, "And of course, you're not going to marry a saint. You know what I mean?" There were also other obstacles in his mind. Judy was nothing like what he had imagined he wanted in a wife. She was uninterested in impressing people and unsupportive of his desire to "run the world." Michael regarded rural North Carolina as home; Judy was firmly rooted in Philadelphia. Because of severe endometriosis, she had had a hysterectomy and was unable to bear children, something Michael had assumed he wanted.

Finally, he adds, "Deep down I couldn't get over the idea, 'Well, maybe she is a zero.' "

Michael explains, "I couldn't make a decision." He realized it wasn't possible to add up the reasons to marry her and the reasons not to marry her to see which list was longer. He knew that type of decision making was not going to work. "It was just too important," he stresses. "So you know, most times, you suddenly find prayer a much more viable option when you need it. Having tried everything else, like going to all the Chinese joints looking for 'Marry her tomorrow' fortune cookies." After months of struggling with the question, Michael recalls, "It just came clear one day. It just was clear. I had been praying no different than otherwise. All I remember about it was, 'I need to ask Judy if she will marry me.' Realizing that was just huge. That was deep. And the first thing I wanted to do was tell somebody so that I couldn't think about it. Because I knew that thinking had been what I was after all along and that after clarity, to put too much thinking on it wasn't going to be good. So I called Mamma and Daddy and told them."

Early the next morning, Michael showed up at Judy's house with a loaf of banana bread and asked her if she wanted to walk to work with him. She agreed, and as they were walking along the Schuylkill River, Judy stopped a moment to clean her glasses. Michael suddenly hugged her, Judy recalls. "Right there, where I happen to have stopped, he had written in the dirt, 'Will you marry me, Judy?' He had ripped off some flowers from behind the art museum and planted them there." Michael gave her a letter and walked a short distance away while she sat down and read it. "It said something to the effect of, 'Will you marry me?

You don't have to give me an answer right away,' " recalls Judy. "And then, we walked the rest of the way to work."

Eight months went by before Judy gave him an answer. Although her attraction to Michael had also been growing, she hadn't seriously thought about marrying him until he proposed, and she had questions of her own. Because of Michael's charisma, Judy wondered, "Would I become a zero just by standing next to him? I think that was my biggest fear. Another was that I didn't know how I'd handle being married, sharing making decisions in that way." In addition, the idea of a single life of service to God still seemed like a possibility for her.

"Having consciously decided ahead of time it's okay if I don't get married helped a lot," says Judy. "It wasn't like, 'This might be your only chance. You better quick say yes.' I think if I was under pressure to get married, I would have felt like, 'Yeah, first thing comes along.' Even if I had married Michael—if I lucked out and Michael was the one who came along—I think entering it with that frame of mind would have been hard on our marriage." Feeling free to consider all options, Judy opened herself to waiting for an answer. "I felt like I was asking God, 'What should I do?' And I was hoping God would say yes," she says with a quiet giggle. "I was. Then one day, I just felt really, really reassured, like everything would be all right. 'Go ahead. Yes is the right thing to say, and everything will be all right.'

"I don't know exactly what I was doing, but people call it praying. I don't really understand what praying is," says Judy. "I was just waiting for an answer to come to me. But I wasn't sitting back waiting. I was leaning forward in my seat waiting." Judy says she is unsure about describing her experience in terms of "God's will." "It seems so presumptuous to say what God wants. I can only describe my end of it, not what's on the other end, whether there's a God out there responding to me. I only know that I was waiting, and I felt an answer would somehow come to me."

Michael is much more comfortable speaking of God as the answerer. Through the months of waiting for Judy's response, he says he was not worried. "By then, I knew that Judy wasn't a saint, but I knew that God and Judy had a good thing going. If Judy said yes, then I knew that it was God's will. And if Judy said no—I also wasn't worried if the answer was no. I would be very, very peaceful about that. That was real, real clear to me all the way through."

Judy's yes finally came. Now, four years after their wedding, they are foster parents, a type of service Judy says she wouldn't have considered had she remained single. Speaking of their family, Michael adds, "It's real clear to me all the time, in a wonderful way, that this is what I'm alive for. When that's working, that feeds the other things. I realize that, left to my own devices, I never would have chosen anything that I've got. The things that are blessings in my life are just blessings, and the more often I try to make blessings happen, the less they happen. So you know, discerning or whatever, I'm sure that's what I've done, but I don't know that that discernment created any of the blessings."

EILEEN AND TOM

Tom and I were friends for about eight months before he left active ministry in the priesthood to test the new direction to which he felt he was being called. He wanted to continue working for social justice, and the job that materialized happened to be thirty miles from where I was living at the time. The distance enabled us to see each other once or twice a week and develop a romantic relationship gradually, which was important since Tom was still confirming the rightness of his decision and had not yet made his resignation from the priesthood permanent. "It was important for me to know that even if things with Eileen didn't work out, I still wouldn't go back," explains Tom. "I didn't want to look back and wonder if the relationship had caused me to leave the priesthood, so I wanted the two decisions to be separate." Six months after his move, Tom finalized his resignation from the priesthood. A few months later, we began to talk seriously about marriage.

Because of my continuing intuition that we would marry, I assumed I was basically waiting for Tom to be ready. I discovered, however, that even with a deep sense of clarity about the direction in which we were moving, I still had feelings to sift through before I felt completely at peace. My dreams were helpful in this process, beginning with a series of dreams about letting go. In each of the dreams there was a man I had known and at some point felt attracted to, and in each one I either said good-bye to the man or introduced him to Tom. The dreams were a powerful reminder that saying yes to one person also meant saying no to other possibilities—not just other romantic possibilities, but also the places and lifestyles these men represented in my imagination.

A few weeks after these dreams, Tom and I went for a walk along a country road and sat down at an abandoned fruit stand. Tom had just returned from a weekend silent retreat where he said he realized he was starting to get "really ready." I smiled although I felt the invisible hand of fear tighten around my throat. Like Nancy in the jewelry shop, I suddenly realized that I might actually get what I most wanted. To symbolize that we felt one step closer to "taking the plunge," Tom and I held hands and jumped off the back of the fruit stand.

That night, I dreamt I was taking a cruise to someplace very far away. Just before the ship was about to take off, I started thinking about how much this trip would cost and wondered if it was too expensive. I ran to my travel agent and asked if I could cancel the trip. She looked puzzled and alarmed and said it was too late to cancel. I had already paid the fare. I awoke feeling trapped and anxious. I interpreted this dream to be about my fear of what marriage would cost me as an individual, a fear that was being drawn to the surface by Tom's new readiness. Writing in my journal and sharing these feelings with Tom, my anxiety gradually evaporated as I realized I was not trapped. I could still say no to the marriage boat, but I didn't want to. What remained true was the continuing intuition that marrying Tom was the right thing to do.

A few weeks later, Tom suggested that we make Lent, which had just begun, a special time to hold our decision in prayer. We decided to spend a half hour in silence every evening and then, at the end of the forty-day season, if we felt clear to do so, we would get engaged on Holy Saturday and tell our families on Easter Sunday. This nonbinding deadline turned out to be very helpful. We had a period of time to test our commitment to each other (one of the functions of engagement) before people started asking, "When's the wedding?" and "What are you going to wear?" And we didn't need to wonder who should propose to whom; we would each have the chance to ask and be asked.

On Holy Saturday, we took a daylong retreat at a local monastery. During the time we spent alone, I wrote in my journal about the parts of me that were dying—the independent traveler of my youth, the awkward high school girl who feared she would never be loved, the woman who preferred to hide her vulnerabilities—and the new life that was beginning. During the time we spent together, Tom and I talked about important events in our pasts and our dreams for the future. At the end of the day, we proposed to each other and exchanged engagement presents. Then we celebrated Easter.

Although the day we got engaged was special and important, it was just one of a series of leaps, like the jump off the back of the fruit stand. We soon had to decide when, where, and how to marry, decisions that symbolized deeper questions about our new life together. These decisions—from the religious traditions in the ceremony to the type of food at the reception—were a wonderful opportunity to practice joint decision making, and I found that the planning actually went better when I viewed it as marital preseason training. Engagement was also a stage of expanding our relationship to include family and friends, integrating each other more fully into our lives. Gathering people for our wedding ceremony and making vows in their presence were integral steps in the transformation. We had a sense of being joined by something greater than our own desires.

Our wedding was certainly a threshold, a crossing over into a new way of life, but the wedding was in no way the end of the journey. I don't feel that I got married one sunny August day; I feel I became married over a period of months. Our wedding was not the end of our mutual discernment; it was a commitment to continue practicing mutual discernment, to nurturing each other's life and growth, to loving in an ongoing way.

Conclusion: Continuing to Grow as a Lover

*W*hen Sarah met Ned thirty-two years ago, she felt he was an answer to her prayers. Thirty-seven-year-old Sarah had spent the summer praying for direction in her life, since she was between jobs and needed to make some important decisions. She wanted to marry and have a child, but she felt open to whatever God had in store for her. When Sarah met Ned near the end of the summer, they quickly agreed to marry. Sarah, who was Canadian, easily found a teaching job in the American city where Ned lived despite her lack of U.S. teaching credentials. Ned worked on finalizing the divorce from his first marriage, which had effectively ended in separation seven years earlier. Although Ned's first wife was vengeful and wanted to make divorce difficult for him, the final divorce decree was signed only seventeen days after the hearing. "It was a record," says Sarah. As potential obstacles to their union miraculously cleared, Sarah felt reassured that her marriage to Ned was "given the go ahead by the powers that be."

Both Sarah and Ned were members of the Bahai faith, which emphasizes the essential unity of all religions. Sarah recalls, "Definitely we had laid ourselves open to God's will, and I thought, 'Well, it is for my benefit that this is being done.' But I found out it wasn't." Although Ned's ex-wife had previously demanded custody of their three sons, she suddenly abandoned the boys, leaving Ned and Sarah to raise them. Ned's youngest son was openly hostile to Sarah, believing she was the reason he had lost his mother. The workload and complexity of relationships increased when Sarah gave birth to a daughter, and Sarah remembers many difficult years as the youngest children were growing up. Today, after thirty-two years of marriage, Sarah has a good relationship with all the children, "But it was a long, long, very hard struggle. I think the lesson I got out of it was that yes, you do God's will, but that doesn't mean it's easy. There were parts of the plan I would never have dreamt of or thought to do for myself." She explains seriously, "It isn't as though, if you're doing God's will, it's just all going to be done for you. Something is required of one."

Even when circumstances are not as difficult as Sarah's, marriage still requires something of us. At the very least it requires us to nurture someone else's life and growth along with our own. Seeking the choices that honor God, self, and others expands our capacity to love, but this stretching is sometimes painful. Sarah was given her dream of marriage and motherhood, but she gave at least as much as she received. As she points out, there were many parts of the plan she would never have imagined for herself, a reminder that even marriages made in heaven must be lived on earth. Letting God surprise us means opening ourselves to challenges as well as blessings.

As Michael pointed out in the last chapter, discernment

does not create blessings. It is not a way to manipulate God, a new technique for getting what we want. Discernment is simply a way of opening ourselves to the blessings meant for us. By learning to recognize the unloving impulses within us, as well as the social pressures that fuel our anxiety, we become more likely to hear the deep, true voice within us. Listening to this voice will not help us to acquire love; it will help us be guided by the source of love. Whether we feel led to marriage or to some other way of life, discernment can continue to guide us on our journey.

Although a loving partnership can help us grow spiritually and psychologically, I have argued that we need not wait for a partner to begin this growth. In fact, the search for romantic love itself can be a powerful agent for self-discovery and transformation. Waiting for a relationship to evolve can teach us trust and patience. Listening to a lover's discernment, even when it conflicts with our own, can help us appreciate the mystery of another. And realizing that we cannot make romantic love happen can help us realize the limits of human control, prompting us to seek divine assistance and guidance. When we see the search for romantic love as an opportunity for growth in and of itself, any partnership we develop will be fundamentally different from one born of guerrilla dating tactics or psychological strategies.

The approach to loving presented in this book stands in sharp contrast to the consumer view of love. Instead of seeking the way of life that will give us the most, we search for the path where we can love most fully. Instead of fearing scarcity, we trust in abundance. Instead of putting a partner at the center of our lives, we put God there. This last point is perhaps the most radical. As Thomas Moore writes at the end of Soul Mates, "Relationship to the divine, hardly discussed in these days of personalism and secularism, satisfies the soul in ways that no substitute can touch. We may well be preoccupied with the theme of interpersonal relationship precisely because we are stuck in a shallow pool of love, unable to arrive at the mystic's view in which the divine is the only satisfying lover, the only true soul mate."

The promise "seek and you will find"—used as a section heading in *Searching for Courtship*—originally referred to this infinite, divine love. Yet even a shallow pool can remind us of the boundless depth and motivate us to search for it. The quest for human love, and the living of romantic relationships, can be part of this spiritual search or act as a substitute, depending on our attitude and awareness. Most of us will have moments where we grasp at love, forgetting that love cannot be possessed. If we are aware of them, these moments can strip the false self and help us to grow as a lover. By leading us through our own depth to the other side of self, even the follies and failures of human love can lead us to the fountainhead, the source of all real loving.

Notes

Introduction

Page 1 *"divert you from your . . ."* Winnifred B. Cutler, Ph.D., *Searching for Courtship: The Smart Woman's Guide to Finding a Good Husband* (New York: Villard Books, 1993), 103.

Page 3 *"The trick is to have . . ."* Judith Sills, Ph.D., *How to Stop Looking for Someone Perfect and Find Someone to Love* (New York: Ballantine Books, 1984), 47.

Chapter One

Page 11 *"What is an advertiser's . . ."* Milton Fisher, *Haven't You Been Single Long Enough? A Practical Guide for Men or Women Who Want to Get Married* (Green Farms, Conn.: Wildcat, 1992), 163.

Page 11 "*It's nothing more than . . .*" William Novak, *The Great American Man Shortage and Other Roadblocks to Romance* (New York: Rawson Associates, 1983), 123.

Page 11 "*Wake up! . . .*" Margaret Kent, *How to Marry the Man of Your Choice* (New York: Warner Books, 1984), 12.

Page 12 "*In reality, there exists . . .*" Erich Fromm, *To Have or to Be* (New York: Harper and Row, 1976), 44. Emphasis in original

Page 12 "Love is the active concern . . ." Erich Fromm, *The Art of Loving* (New York: Harper and Row, 1956), 26. Emphasis in original.

Page 17 "*a marriage truly made . . .*" Ellen Fein and Sherrie Schneider, *The Rules: Time-Tested Secrets for Capturing the Heart of Mr. Right* (New York: Warner Books, 1995), 6.

Page 17 "The Rules *way is not . . .*" Ibid., 147.

Page 18 "*supplanted religion as the arena . . .*" Robert A. Johnson, *We: Understanding the Psychology of Romantic Love* (New York: HarperCollins, 1983), xi.

Page 25 "*The human heart wants . . .*" M. Basil Pennington, *Called: New Thinking on Christian Vocation* (New York: Seabury Press, 1983), 23.

Chapter Two

Page 37 "*. . . love, joy, peace, patience . . .*" Galatians 5:22–23. *The New Oxford Annotated Bible with the Apoc-*

rypha, expanded edition, revised standard version (New York: Oxford University Press, 1977).

Page 37 "If you want the proper results . . ." Thomas Cleary, ed. and trans., *The Spirit of Tao* (Boston and London: Shambhala, 1993), 126–27.

Page 38 "Discernment is a gift . . ." Suzanne G. Farnham et al., *Listening Hearts: Discerning Call in Community* (Harrisburg, Pa.: Morehouse, 1991), 24.

Page 41 "one slot for me . . ." Pennington, *Called: New Thinking on Christian Vocation*, 87–88.

Page 43 "by the door of this . . ." Thomas Merton, *The New Man* (New York: Mentor-Omega Books, 1961), 32.

Page 44 "Before we can realize . . ." Ibid., 73.

Chapter Three

Page 60 "My existence makes people uncomfortable. . . ." Stephanie Brush, "Still Single at 38," *McCall's*, April 1993, 86. Emphasis in original.

Page 61 "ready to marry men . . ." Susan Faludi, *Backlash: The Undeclared War against American Women* (New York: Crown, 1991), 18.

Page 63 "As strong as the yearning . . ." Thomas Moore, *Soul Mates: Honoring the Mysteries of Love and Relationship* (New York: HarperCollins, 1994), 11–12.

Page 68 "while one is consciously afraid . . ." Fromm, *The Art of Loving,* 127. Emphasis in original.

Page 85 *"a good marriage is . . ."* John J. L. Mood, ed., *Rilke on Love and Other Difficulties* (New York: W.W. Norton, 1975), 28.

Chapter Four

Page 102 *"Father, if thou art . . ."* Luke 22:42. *The New Oxford Annotated Bible with the Apocrypha.*

Page 105 *"Your social life . . ."* Sharyn Wolf, *Guerrilla Dating Tactics: Strategies, Tips and Secrets for Finding Romance* (New York: Plume, 1993), 159–60.

Page 105 *"It is not, as some may think . . ."* Thomas W. McKnight and Robert H. Phillips, *More Love Tactics: How to Win That Special Someone* (Garden City Park, N.Y.: Avery, 1993), viii. Emphasis in original.

Page 106 "Passive patience is the . . ." Patricia Allen and Sandra Harman, *Getting to "I Do"* (New York: William Morrow, 1994), 157. Emphasis in original.

Chapter Five

Pages 129–30 *"Ultimately the only enduring . . ."* Johnson, *We: Understanding the Psychology of Romantic Love,* 72, 195, 110.

Page 135 *"once the realization . . ."*Mood, ed., *Rilke on Love and Other Difficulties,* 28. Emphasis in original.

Pages 136–37 "understand the human soul . . ." Erich Fromm, *For the Love of Life*, trans. Robert Kimber and Rita Kimber, ed. Hans Jurgen Schultz (New York: The Free Press, 1986), 67–68. Emphasis in original.

Page 137 "Does he tap his . . ." Tracy Cabot, *How to Make a Man Fall in Love with You* (New York: Dell, 1984), 13, 143, 18.

Pages 137–38 "The heart is a mystery . . ." Moore, *Soul Mates*, xi.

Page 138 "All intimate relationships require . . ." Ibid., 49.

Page 139 "I shall never forget . . ." Nikos Kazantzakis, *Zorba the Greek*, trans. Carl Wildman (New York: Simon and Schuster, 1952), 120–21.

Page 141 "A basic guideline . . ." Robert F. Morneau, *Spiritual Direction: Principles and Practices* (New York: Crossroad, 1994), 42–43.

Chapter Six

Page 161 "Humility, grounded in self-knowledge . . ." Farnham et al., *Listening Hearts*, 33.

Page 168 "the story of God's breakthrough . . ." John A. Sanford, *Dreams: God's Forgotten Language* (New York: Lippincott, 1968), 116, 200, 213.

Page 168 "the dream may be one of the most common avenues . . ." Morton T. Kelsey, *Dreams: A Way to Listen to God* (New York: Paulist Press, 1978), 5.

Page 169 "*A healthy skepticism of our own motives . . .*" Farnham et al., *Listening Hearts*, 45.

Conclusion

Pages 191–92 "*Relationship to the divine . . .*" Moore, *Soul Mates*, 258.

Bibliography

Courtship Advice

Allen, Patricia, and Sandra Harman. *Getting to "I Do."* New York: William Morrow, 1994.

"Are You Meant to Be Married?" *Complete Woman*, February 1995.

Berkowitz, Bob, with Roger Gittines. *What Men Won't Tell You but Women Need to Know.* New York: Avon, 1990.

Bernikow, Louise. "Who Says You Can't Enjoy Sex without Commitment?" *Cosmopolitan*, January 1996.

Blake, George. *Single Again: Dating and Meeting New Friends the Second Time Around.* Saratoga, Calif.: R&E, 1991.

Cabot, Tracy. *How to Make a Man Fall in Love with You.* New York: Dell, 1984.

————. *Marrying Later, Marrying Smarter: How Women over Thirty Can Use Their Savvy and Experience to Attract Exciting, Marriageable Men.* New York: Dell, 1990.

Cutler, Winnifred B., Ph.D. *Searching for Courtship: The Smart Woman's Guide to Finding a Good Husband.* New York: Villard Books, 1993.

De Angelis, Barbara. *Are You the One for Me? Knowing Who's Right and Avoiding Who's Wrong.* New York: Dell, 1992.

De Jongh, Monique Jellerette, and Cassandra Marshall Cata-Louis. *How to Marry a Black Man: The Real Deal.* New York: Doubleday, 1996.

Dominitz, Ben. *How to Find the Love of Your Life.* Rocklin, Calif.: Prima, 1994.

Dormen, Lesley. "Will Your Love Last? Eight Early Clues." *Glamour,* August 1993.

————. "Weekend Panic." *Glamour,* September 1994.

Ellner, Eddie. "Six Things Men Hate." *Mademoiselle,* March 1995.

"Fake a Great Beach Body: 8 Instant Slimming Tricks." *Mademoiselle,* July 1995.

Fein, Ellen, and Sherrie Schneider. *The Rules: Time-Tested Secrets for Capturing the Heart of Mr. Right.* New York: Warner Books, 1995.

Fisher, Milton. *Haven't You Been Single Long Enough? A Practical Guide for Men or Women Who Want to Get Married.* Green Farms, Conn.: Wildcat, 1992.

Forsyth, Sondra. "We're Happy, So Why Won't He Marry Me?" *Mademoiselle*, July 1994.

Gallatin, Martin V., Ph.D. *How to Get Married in a Year or Less.* New York: S.P.I. Books, 1991.

Gerosa, Melina. "Is This the Man You Want to Marry?" *Cosmopolitan*, November 1993.

Glanz, Larry, and Robert H. Phillips. *How to Start a Romantic Encounter.* Garden City Park, N.Y.: Avery, 1993.

Glatzer, Randi. "Where the Men Are." *Mademoiselle*, February 1995.

"Hooking Him." *American Woman*, January/February 1995.

"How to Put a Man under Your Spell in 10 Loving Steps." *Complete Woman*, February 1995.

Jacoby, Susan. "The Pressure to Have a Baby." *Glamour*, September 1995.

Jenkins, Karen. *Chronically Single Women: How to Get out of the Singles Trap.* Deerfield Beach, Fla.: Health Communications, 1994.

Kent, Margaret. *How to Marry the Man of Your Choice.* New York: Warner Books, 1984.

Kreidman, Ellen. *Light His Fire: How to Keep Your Man Passionately and Hopelessly in Love with You.* New York: Dell, 1989.

Kuriansky, Judy, Ph.D. *How to Love a Nice Guy.* New York: Doubleday, 1990.

Lederman, Ellen. *The Best Places to Meet Good Men.* Rocklin, Calif.: Prima, 1991.

Lemon, Kevin. *Were You Born for Each Other? Finding, Catching, and Keeping the Love of Your Life.* New York: Delacorte Press, 1991.

"Marry Me or Else!" *American Woman,* January/February 1996.

Masterton, Graham. *Single, Wild, Sexy . . . and Safe: The Single Woman's Up-to-Date Guide to Finding a Mate and Making Her Most Intimate Uninhibited Erotic Dreams Come True.* New York: Signet, 1994.

———. "Men Who Make the Best Lovers." *Women's Own,* November 1995.

McKnight, Thomas W., and Robert H. Phillips. *Love Tactics: How to Win the One You Want.* Garden City Park, N.Y.: Avery, 1988.

———. *More Love Tactics: How to Win That Special Someone.* Garden City Park, N.Y.: Avery, 1993.

Nelson, Sara. "Shopping for a Man." *Glamour,* March 1992.

Novak, William. *The Great American Man Shortage and Other Roadblocks to Romance.* New York: Rawson Associates, 1983.

Page, Susan. *If I'm So Wonderful, Why Am I Still Single?* New York: Bantam Books, 1990.

Rabin, Susan, with Barbara Lazowski. *How to Attract Anyone, Anytime, Anyplace: The Smart Guide to Flirting.* New York: Plume, 1993.

Rich, Hillary. *Get Married Now: The Definitive Guide for Finding and Marrying the Right Mate for You.* Holbrook, Mass.: Bob Adams, 1993.

Rich, Katherine Russell. "How to Date Like a Manager." *Glamour,* September 1992.

Rodriguez, Alicia. "Are You Getting Enough from Your Guy?" *Mademoiselle,* March 1994.

Sayles, Ginie Polo. *How to Marry the Rich.* New York: Berkley Books, 1992.

Schappel, Elissa. "Why Bitchy Women Get the Best Men." *Marie Claire,* April 1996.

Sills, Judith, Ph.D. *How to Stop Looking for Someone Perfect and Find Someone to Love.* New York: Ballantine Books, 1984.

————. *A Fine Romance: The Passage of Courtship from Meeting to Marriage.* New York: Ballantine Books, 1987.

Sterling, A. Justin. *What Really Works with Men*. New York: Warner Books, 1992.

Ullman, Jeffrey. "How to Meet the Man of Your Dreams." *American Woman*, September/October 1995.

Warren, Neil Clark, Ph.D. *Find the Love of Your Life: Ten Principles for Choosing the Right Marriage Partner*. Colorado Springs, Colo.: Focus on the Family, 1992.

Welty, Ellen. "It's Their Wedding and I'll Cry If I Want To." *Mademoiselle*, May 1991.

Wolf, Sharyn. *Guerrilla Dating Tactics: Strategies, Tips and Secrets for Finding Romance*. New York: Plume, 1993.

Wolf, Sharyn, with Katy Koontz. *50 Ways to Find a Lover: Proven Techniques for Finding Someone Special*. Holbrook, Mass.: Bob Adams, 1992.

Other Sources

Anderson, Sherry Ruth, and Patricia Hopkins. *The Feminine Face of God: The Unfolding of the Sacred in Women*. New York: Bantam Books, 1992.

Boulding, Elise. *One Small Plot of Heaven: Reflections on Family Life by a Quaker Sociologist*. Wallingford, Pa.: Pendle Hill, 1989.

Brush, Stephanie. "Still Single at 38." *McCall's*, April 1993.

Campbell, Joseph, ed. *The Portable Jung*. New York: Penguin Books, 1976.

Cleary, Thomas, ed. and trans. *The Spirit of Tao*. Boston: Shambhala, 1993.

Faludi, Susan. *Backlash: The Undeclared War against American Women*. New York: Crown, 1991.

Farnham, Suzanne G., Joseph P. Gill, R. Taylor McLean, and Susan M. Ward. *Listening Hearts: Discerning Call in Community*. Harrisburg, Pa.: Morehouse, 1991.

Finley, James. *Merton's Palace of Nowhere: A Search for God through Awareness of the True Self*. Notre Dame, Ind.: Ave Maria Press, 1978.

Foundation for Inner Peace. *A Course in Miracles*, second edition. New York: Viking, 1996.

Frankl, Viktor E. *Man's Search for Meaning*. New York: Pocket Books, 1959.

Freedman, Rita, Ph.D. *Bodylove: Learning to Like Our Looks and Ourselves*. New York: Harper and Row, 1988.

Friedan, Betty. *The Second Stage*. New York: Summit Books, 1981.

Fromm, Erich. *The Art of Loving*. New York: Harper and Row, 1956.

————. *To Have or to Be?* New York: Harper and Row, 1976.

Haughey, John C., S.J. *Should Anyone Say Forever: On Making, Keeping and Breaking Commitments.* Garden City, N.Y.: Doubleday, 1975.

Hendrix, Harville, Ph.D. *Getting the Love You Want: A Guide for Couples.* New York: Harper Perennial, 1990.

————. *Keeping the Love You Find: A Guide for Singles.* New York: Pocket Books, 1992.

Higgins, John J., S.J. *Thomas Merton on Prayer.* Garden City, N.Y.: Doubleday, 1973.

Hirschmann, Jane R., and Carol H. Munter. *When Women Stop Hating Their Bodies: Freeing Yourself from Food and Weight Obsession.* New York: Fawcett Columbine, 1995.

Ignatius of Loyola. *The Spiritual Exercises of St. Ignatius.* Translated by George E. Ganss, S.J. St. Louis: The Institute of Jesuit Sources, 1992.

Johnson, Robert A. *We: Understanding the Psychology of Romantic Love.* New York: HarperCollins, 1983.

Kazantzakis, Nikos. *Zorba the Greek.* Translated by Carl Wildman. New York: Simon and Schuster, 1952.

Kelsey, Morton T. *God, Dreams, and Revelation: Christian Interpretation of Dreams.* Minneapolis, Minn.: Augsburg, 1974.

————. *Dreams: A Way to Listen to God*. New York: Paulist Press, 1978.

Kelsey, Morton, and Barbara Kelsey. *Sacrament of Sexuality: The Spirituality and Psychology of Sex*. Rockport, Mass.: Element, 1991.

Kidd, Sue Monk. *When the Heart Waits: Spiritual Direction for Life's Sacred Questions*. San Francisco, Calif.: Harper and Row, 1990.

Lerner, Harriet Goldhor, Ph.D. *The Dance of Intimacy: A Woman's Guide to Courageous Acts of Change in Key Relationships*. New York: Harper and Row, 1989.

————. *The Dance of Deception: Pretending and Truth-Telling in Women's Lives*. New York: HarperCollins, 1993.

Lewis, C. S. *The Four Loves*. New York: Harvest, 1960.

Loring, Patricia. *Spiritual Discernment*. Pendle Hill Pamphlet 305. Wallingford, Pa.: Pendle Hill Publications, 1992.

Lovenheim, Barbara. *Beating the Marriage Odds: When You Are Smart, Single, and over 35*. New York: William Morrow, 1990.

May, Rollo. *Love and Will*. New York: W.W. Norton, 1969.

Merton, Thomas. *No Man Is an Island*. San Diego: Harvest, 1955.

————. *The New Man*. New York: Mentor-Omega Books, 1961.

Mood, John J. L. *Rilke on Love and Other Difficulties: Translations and Considerations of Rainer Maria Rilke*. New York: W.W. Norton, 1975.

Moore, Thomas. *Soul Mates: Honoring the Mysteries of Love and Relationship*. New York: HarperCollins, 1994.

Morley, Barry. *Beyond Consensus: Salvaging Sense of the Meeting*. Pendle Hill Pamphlet 307. Wallingford, Pa.: Pendle Hill Publications, 1993.

Morneau, Robert F. *Spiritual Direction: Principles and Practices*. New York: Crossroad, 1994.

Muto, Susan Annette. *Celebrating the Single Life: A Spirituality for Single Persons in Today's World*. Garden City, N.Y.: Doubleday, 1982.

Nelson, James B., and Sandra P. Longfellow, eds. *Sexuality and the Sacred: Sources for Theological Reflection*. Louisville, Ky.: Westminster/John Knox Press, 1994.

The New Oxford Annotated Bible with the Apocrypha. Expanded Edition, Revised Standard Version. New York: Oxford University Press, 1977.

Nouwen, Henri. *Reaching Out: The Three Movements of the Spiritual Life*. Garden City, N.Y.: Image Books, Doubleday, 1975.

————. *Clowning in Rome: Reflections on Solitude, Celibacy, Prayer, and Contemplation*. Garden City, N.Y.: Image Books, Doubleday, 1979.

Peck, M. Scott, M.D. *A World Waiting to Be Born: Civility Rediscovered*. New York: Bantam Books, 1993.

Pennington, M. Basil. *Called: New Thinking on Christian Vocation*. New York: Seabury Press, 1983.

Russionoff, Penelope, Ph.D. *Why Do I Think I Am Nothing without a Man?* New York: Bantam Books, 1981.

Sanford, John A. *Dreams: God's Forgotten Language*. New York: Lippincott, 1968.

Savary, Louis M., Patricia H. Berne, and Strephon Kaplan Williams. *Dreams and Spiritual Growth: A Christian Approach to Dreamwork*. New York: Paulist Press, 1984.

Sheeran, Michael J. *Beyond Majority Rule: Voteless Decisions in the Religious Society of Friends*. Philadelphia, Pa.: Philadelphia Yearly Meeting, 1983.

Teresa of Avila. *The Interior Castle*. Edited and translated by E. Allison Peers. Garden City, N.Y.: Image, Doubleday, 1961.

Wehr, Demaris S. *Jung and Feminism: Liberating Archetypes*. Boston: Beacon Press, 1987.

Welwood, John, ed. *Challenge of the Heart: Love, Sex and Intimacy in Changing Times*. Boston: Shambhala, 1985.

Wolf, Naomi. *The Beauty Myth: How Images of Beauty Are Used against Women*. New York: William Morrow, 1991.

———. *Promiscuities: The Secret Struggle for Womanhood*. New York: Random House, 1997.

Wolfe, Leanna. *Women Who May Never Marry: The Reasons, Realities, and Opportunities*. Atlanta, Ga.: Longstreet, 1993.